THE HARMONY WITHIN

Other books by Rolland Hein:

Christian Mythmakers: Lewis, L'Engle, Tolkien & Others

Life Essential: The Hope of the Gospel, ed.

Creation in Christ: The Unspoken Sermons of George MacDonald, ed.

George MacDonald's World: An Anthology from the Novels, ed.

The Miracles of Our Lord, ed.

George MacDonald: Victorian Mythmaker

The Heart of George MacDonald, ed.

THE
*H*ARMONY
*W*ITHIN

THE SPIRITUAL VISION OF

GEORGE MACDONALD

Revised Edition

Rolland Hein

Cornerstone Press Chicago
Chicago, Illinois

Published by Cornerstone Press Chicago
939 W. Wilson Ave.
Chicago, IL 60640
www.cornerstonepress.com
cspress@jpusa.chi.il.us

Cover design by Pat Peterson/*wheatsdesign*
The author and publisher would like to thank Johnson
Reprints (a division of Harcourt Brace Jovanovich) for permis-
sion to use the cover photo and reprint excerpts from Greville
MacDonald's *George MacDonald & His Wife* (1971).

Printed in the United States of America
03 02 01 00 99   5 4 3 2 1

ISBN 0-940895-43-9

Library of Congress Cataloging-in-Publication Data

Hein, Rolland.
    The harmony within: the spiritual vision of George MacDonald /
Rolland Hein.
        p.   cm.
    Includes bibliographical references (p.   ) and index.
    ISBN 0-940895-43-9
    MacDonald George. 1824-1905—Criticism and interpretation.
2. Christianity and literature—Scotland—History—19th century.
3. Christian fiction, English—Scottish Authors—History and
criticism. 4. Fantasy fiction, Scottish—History and criticism.
5. Spiritual life in literature.   I. Title.
PR4969.H44   1999
823'. 8—dc21
                                                    99–31519
                                                      CIP

To Mother and Dad

*From whom I first learned to
love the good and the true*

Contents

ACKNOWLEDGMENTS

Portions of this book have appeared in somewhat altered form in *Faith in Fiction: A Study of the Effects of Religious Convictions in the Adult Fantasies and Novels of George MacDonald*, Diss. Purdue University, 1971; "Lilith: Theology through Mythopoeia," *Christian Scholar's Review*, 3 (1974), 215-231; and "If You Would But Write Novels, Mr. MacDonald," *Seven*, 1 (1980), 11-27. Reprinted by permission. I am indebted to Joshua Breithaupt for doing much work on "The Glossary of Scottish Terms."

Introduction

⊕ "WHERE ARE YE GOING?" a voice with a strong Scotch accent inquires of the narrator in C. S. Lewis's *The Great Divorce*, a fantasy of heaven and hell. The narrator, wandering through the nether world, tells how he turned to see an "enthroned and shining god, whose ageless spirit weighed upon mine like a burden of solid gold: and yet, at the very same moment, here was an old weather-beaten man, one who might have been a shepherd." When the inquirer identifies himself as George MacDonald, the narrator is beside himself with joy. He cries, "'Then you can tell me! You at least will not deceive me.'" He continues:

> I tried, trembling, to tell this man all that his writings had done for me. I tried to tell how a certain frosty afternoon at Leatherhead Station when I first bought a copy of *Phantastes* (being then about sixteen years old) had been to me what the first sight of Beatrice had been to Dante: Here begins the New Life. I started to confess how long that Life had delayed in the region of imagination merely: how slowly and reluctantly I had come to admit that his Christendom had

> more than an accidental connexion with it, how hard
> I had tried not to see that the true name of the qual-
> ity which first met me in his books is Holiness. [1]

After humbly receiving this homage, MacDonald becomes the narrator's teacher, explaining to him many difficult truths about heaven and hell.

Lewis chose his guide well. He owed George MacDonald a large spiritual debt, and, in his many writings, often acknowledged MacDonald as his master. C. S. Lewis is, of course, one of the leading Christian apologists of the twentieth century. These two men never met, Lewis's life spanning the first two-thirds of his century and MacDonald's the latter three-fourths of the nineteenth, but MacDonald wrote prolifically and Lewis became quite familiar with his work.

As Lewis's narrator states, his first encounter with the holiness that MacDonald defines began in the realm of the imagination and from there began to permeate his life. MacDonald knew that the best way to connect people with eternity was to nourish their imaginations:

> In very truth, a wise imagination, which is the
> presence of the spirit of God, is the best guide that
> man or woman can have; for it is not the things we see
> the most clearly that influence us the most
> powerfully; undefined, yet vivid visions of something
> beyond, something which eye has not seen nor ear
> heard, have far more influence than any logical

---

1. *The Great Divorce* (New York: Macmillan, 1946), 60–61. Italics his. For Lewis's more complete explanation of his debt to MacDonald, see *Surprised by Joy* (New York: Harcourt, 1955), and the Preface to *George MacDonald: An Anthology* (New York: Macmillan, 1948), 10–22, hereafter cited as *Anthology*. The latter is an excellent summary of MacDonald's life and achievement.

sequences whereby the same things may be demonstrated to the intellect.[2]

Stories that present "vivid visions" of things not seen but deeply felt are properly called myths. In vivid contrast to literature assuming the soul's mortality, Christian myths suppose the immortality of the soul and view all human experience from the vantage point of transcendence.

Many readers of MacDonald's fantasies are profoundly moved by them, and they are curious about the source and nature of this influence. What affects them are images that entice by their vague symbolic suggestions of something beyond time, both ineffable and momentous, that beckons and allures. In the fairy story *The Golden Key* the main character finds a magnificent key at the foot of a rainbow in Fairyland. Puzzled by its purpose, he spends his life searching for what it will unlock, discovering in the end that it opens a jeweled gate into eternity. The key is an apt symbol of whatever it is that compels people upon quests for which temporal rewards are woefully inadequate. To undertake to allegorize it would be to diminish greatly its impact. It is the power of myth that rivets our attention; "MacDonald is the greatest genius of this kind whom I know," C. S. Lewis affirmed.[3]

The holiness that Lewis found in MacDonald's writings is a vision of what life ought to be. George MacDonald not only discerned compellingly the nature of moral and spiritual well-being, his writings create

2. "The Imagination: Its Function and Culture," *A Dish of Orts*, 28. Hereafter cited as *ADO*.
3. "Preface," *Anthology*, 16.

within his readers strong desires towards it. "I try to show what we might be, may be, must be, shall be—and something of the struggle to gain it," he affirmed.[4] His understanding of what the lives of people should be stands in contrast to what so many people seem to want—a sensual paradise, painless and troublefree, in which moral restrictions are irrelevant to private behavior. Such a world realized would in fact be one of sterility, oppressive conformity, and mind-wrenching boredom. No matter how skeptical the contemporary mind may be, something within the human heart still longs for the right and the good. Few writers appeal to that longing; MacDonald does.

"His main forte was fantasy," Maurice Sendak explains. "For admirers of MacDonald, such as myself, his work has something of the effect of a hallucinatory drug. Finishing one of his stories is often like waking from a dream—one's own dream."[5] MacDonald's writings create within the reader an enriched state of consciousness, one in which the attention is focused upon the anagogic level of life, that is, those attitudes and actions that are eternally significant. Readers are made to dismiss materialistic preoccupations—anxieties about, (to paraphrase Christ) what we shall eat or what we shall drink, or about our bodies, what we shall put on—in favor of a vision of the eternally Real. MacDonald's myths do not create other worlds so much as they enable us to understand the true realities of this

4. Letter to William Mount-Temple, 13 January 1879, The National Library of Scotland.
5. *Worlds of Childhood: The Art and Craft of Writing of Children*, William Zinsser, ed. (Boston: Houghton Mifflin, 1990), 188.

day's events and enable us to meet them with peace, joy, and a greater determination to walk worthy of the grace bestowed upon our lives.

MacDonald accomplishes his task largely through story. Though Lewis was an atheistic rationalist when he first read *Phantastes*, what so deeply affected him was not argument but a fantasy, one that aroused within him longings that he later recognized could only have satisfaction beyond this life. MacDonald's faith in this type of story or myth was strong. He understood its potential to arouse "a trouble that has no name—the trouble of wanting one knows not what—or how to seek it."[6]

Since he found that the fantasies he most enjoyed writing were of little interest to his public and did not sell, the practical necessity of earning a living prompted him to write novels. Although he was unable to interest any publisher in his initial manuscript, he tried again and in 1863 published *David Elginbrod.* Building on its success, he brought out some two dozen more during his lifetime. MacDonald's accomplishment in these is to lift realistic portrayals of life to the level of anagogic significance by investing them with a mythic tone. W. H. Auden wrote: "To me, George MacDonald's most extraordinary, and precious, gift is his ability, in all his stories, to create an atmosphere of goodness about which there is nothing phony or moralistic."[7] While MacDonald's fantasies are more purely mythic, his novels offer the reader a vision of life enriched by the illumination a mythic vision affords. At every turn, eternity is present in time.

6. *Robert Falconer,* Chapter 14.
7. *The Cool Web: The Pattern of Children's Reading,* Margaret Meeks, Aidan Warlow, Griselda Barton, eds. (New York: Atheneum, 1978), 105.

MacDonald's art is not allegorical, if by that term one means the rather rigid and mechanical relations between select images and their abstract significances that one finds, say, in *The Pilgrim's Progress*. Because the ultimate realities he is often pursuing imaginatively are elusive and obscure, existing without any specific counterpart in human experience, no metaphors suffice; they can only be suggested through vaguely symbolic images. Such symbols do not—cannot—capture or imprison the realities to which they point. To define them precisely would be to intellectualize their meaning entirely, something impossible by the very nature of things. Mere rational analysis upon myth is severely limited.

Further, interpretations may vary from person to person. We see according to our natures and capacities. MacDonald was fully aware of this. To the objection: "But a man may then imagine in your work what he pleases, what you never meant!" MacDonald replies: "Not what he pleases, but what he can. If he be not a true man, he will draw evil out of the best. . . . If he be a true man, he will imagine true things; what matter whether I meant them or not?" He felt his task in writing mythopoeia was not to give his readers something to think about, but rather "to wake things up" within them, to arouse "the something deeper than the understanding—the power that underlies thoughts."[8] Readers should allow his stories to work upon them as he intended; the experience should not be unlike listening to a piece of classical music.

8. "The Fantastic Imagination," *ADO*. This essay is currently available in *The Heart of George MacDonald*, Rolland Hein ed., (Wheaton, Ill: Harold Shaw, 1994), 423–28.

However, the direct statements he makes in his many novels and published sermons indicate he was deeply concerned to give his hearers "something to think about." Being the earnest Christian that he was, his mythic writings are inevitably shaped by his deepest convictions. This study undertakes to show how his convictions shaped his art. It does not aim to replace or discredit in readers' minds the significances they may see for themselves. Such meanings may stand at considerable distance from MacDonald's conscious purposes, but, nevertheless, be for a particular reader more pertinent than those the author intended. Nor does it imply that the chief value of reading MacDonald's work lies in an intellectual grasp of his theological positions.

A knowledge of the ideas that conceived the images, however, deepens one's appreciation for how aptly MacDonald's theology applies to human experience. For instance, if one views the image of a fire burning in the shape of beautiful roses—as does the great-great-grandmother's fire in *The Princess and the Goblin*—in the light of the sermon "The Consuming Fire," one understands it as suggesting something otherwise unstateable about the nature of God's holy love: it is at once painful and beautiful in its purifying effects. In its suggestive vagueness the scene wields a power more direct than what allegory can achieve.

For various reasons George MacDonald was disillusioned with the work of most Christian theologians and would subscribe completely to no theological system. He was throughout his life, however, a careful and devout student of the Bible. Attracted to texts too often ignored by theological systematizers, his conclusions were thought heterodox by those convinced of a dogmatic theology, who saw Christian truth as primarily propositional, but he held to nothing that he could not justify from Scripture. He tried carefully to avoid controversy, for he felt argument futile. He was not interested in disturbing anyone whose theology, however different from his, was producing a life of joyous righteousness. His concern was with those who demurred in the presence of the Christianity to which they had been exposed, feeling it an inadequate explanation for human experience, yet who felt a dissatisfaction within their beings and longed for truth. "It is impossible to know God as he is and not believe in him," MacDonald said. The imaginative power endemic in the mythic embodiments of his thought depicts the truths he saw.

It should be emphasized, therefore, lest any misunderstand, that the fantasies are not anecdotes and illustrations of another theological system; at their best they are imaginative and symbolic explorations of a vision of the significance of life here and hereafter. Although one readily acknowledges that much of his art is too overtly didactic, his best imaginative writings are artistic in a high sense of the term. Emotions are not simply described to us; they are created within us. We are made to feel awe in the depths of our beings. The effects that one experiences are those that great myths have always created within people. This is not to say that MacDonald's writings are a sacred revelation, but it is to suggest that open-minded readers may well have moments when they feel more near the ultimately Real than they have yet been.

When a given story achieved mythic quality, MacDonald was fond of referring to it as containing a "central spot of red." Writing to his wife on one occasion, he complained to her of the quality of certain stories he happened to be reading, and explained: "As stories they just want the one central spot of red—the wonderful thing which, whether in a fairy story or a world or a human being is the life—depth—whether of truth or humour or pathos—the eye to the face of it—the thing that shows the unshowable. . . ."[9] It is with these "spots of red" in MacDonald's own writings that we are especially concerned in this present volume, as we consider the separate stories and their themes.

Good criticism operates upon the faith that what it is able to accomplish is at best but an aid to the reader's more complete experience of the primary work itself; it never sees itself as a substitute for that experience. Therefore, this present work, though it endeavors to be a self-sufficient piece of criticism, fails seriously to achieve its purpose whenever it may be used by someone as a means of "understanding MacDonald's message" without reading the stories firsthand. I offer this exposition because these works by George MacDonald, read by themselves, may strike many readers as being too recondite and obscure. But readers must first have seen, however dimly, the red spot glowing in the tale as it is being read, else they will never really know the thrill of that encounter.

9. George MacDonald to Louisa, n.d. (but written early in 1861), The MacDonald Collection, The Beinecke Rare Book and Manuscript Library.

Chapter 1

"Corage! God Mend Al!"

"'All a man has to do, is to better what he can.'"
—the knight in *Phantastes*

A NOTICEABLE TENSION EXISTS between the above title and epigraph. The title is an anagram, formed from the letters of George MacDonald's name, which he used as his family motto. It suggests his strong confidence in the purpose of God ultimately to overrule all evil and recompense all suffering. But MacDonald also saw man not as a passive beneficiary of this process, but as a cocreator, enlisted by God to have a large share in the creative process whereby good is realized. Both MacDonald's life and his writings evidence the strength with which he held each of these convictions, and the success with which he blended them.

George MacDonald was born on December 10, 1824, at Huntly, in Aberdeenshire, Scotland.[1] The history of

1. Greville MacDonald, *George MacDonald and His Wife* (1924);

the area is rich with tales of warring clans, treacherous massacres, vicious hatreds, and deep loyalties. Huntly is a small town situated in a valley, with the River Bogie running through it, and the ancient Huntly Castle standing nearby. The people are staunch Celts whose stern outlook on life was molded, in MacDonald's time, by the hardships of peasant farming and the flax and wool weaving industries. Religiously, they adhered sternly to John Knox's Calvinism.

MACDONALD'S FATHER

When George MacDonald was eight his mother died of tuberculosis, the same disease that persistently claimed a large number of family members throughout MacDonald's lifetime, including four of his own children. Although the grandmother was nearby and his new stepmother was kindly and compassionate, he looked to his father to be both father and mother to him, and the two established a strong and loving bond.[2] As a young man MacDonald wrote letters to his father, consulting him on his main decisions and confiding in him his thoughts and opinions—letters which are a rich source of material on MacDonald's personal life and thought.

Whitehorn,Calif.: Johannesen, 1998) is an early source of biographical material. Hereafter cited as *GMDW*. Greville also makes some references to his father in his autobiography *Reminiscences of a Specialist* (London: George Allen & Unwin, 1932), hereafter cited as *ROS*. Ronald MacDonald, *From a Northern Window* (1911, Eureka,Calif.: Sunrise, 1989), is a sensitive tribute. Rolland Hein, *George MacDonald: Victorian Mythmaker* (1993; Whitehorn,Calif.: Johannesen, 1999) is a complete biography based on Greville's work, family letters, and other available materials.

2. See Lewis, *Anthology*, 10–11. Woolf, *GK*, 13–15, rejects this view, finding instead repressed rebelliousness and guilt in MacDonald's relationship with his father.

Greville MacDonald records a great many of these letters.

Greville depicts George MacDonald, Sr., as a man of legendary toughness. He records of his grandfather with pride:

> In 1825 my grandfather's left leg was amputated above the knee for white swelling, as tuberculous disease of the joint was then named, two years previous treatment with blisters and seton having proved unsuccessful. My father was told by the doctor who operated—it being before the days of chloroform—how the patient refused the customary stupefying dose of whisky, or even to have his face covered, preferring to watch the operation; and that only for one moment, when the knife first transfixed the flesh, did he turn his face away and ejaculate a faint, sibilant "whiff." (*GMDW*, 34)

This stern fiber was balanced by a sense of humor and capacity for understanding his family. Family life, according to Greville, was idyllic:

> Sufficient discipline ruled the home. A look of displeasure from the beloved father was punishment for any sin, while his rebuke was awful indeed. Any complaints against their wild escapades, unless involving disobedience, he would smile at, though he might warn and restrict. There was plenty for the hungriest boys of all that was necessary—except, to be sure, oxygen indoors; but clothes were mostly shabby, and the money was always scarce. On the other hand there were cattle in the byre, horses in the stable, wild

> bees' nests in the stone dykes, whose honeycomb
> eaten like bread was a priceless joy. . . . (*GMDW,* 54)

The tone here is obviously glowing. The point is that
George MacDonald's perception of his father, both in
boyhood and in manhood, was a continual source of
admiration and delight to him. This relationship shaped
MacDonald's understanding of the Fatherhood of God.
Compared to the spiritual beauty of George MacDonald
Sr., the wrathful heavenly father of many Scottish
Calvinists seemed far inferior. The strong yet loving and
sympathetic fathers that people MacDonald's fiction are
modeled in large part on his own father.

RELIGIOUS BACKGROUND

The religious convictions of MacDonald's family were
strict. His grandmother was famous for her narrow piety:
she even committed her son's violin to the flames, lest
playing it be detrimental to his faith and that of others.
The family was deeply involved in the Evangelical
movement that gave birth to the Scottish Free Church in
1843. The issues that prompted the formation of the Free
Church, however, had considerably more to do with
church government than with doctrine. The Scottish
Presbyterianism that ruled in MacDonald's boyhood
home maintained essentially the rigid Calvinist doctrines
of its founder, John Knox. It was Knox, himself a student
of John Calvin, who brought the Reformation to
Scotland in the middle of the sixteenth century. His
convictions, elaborated in the strongly worded
Westminster Confession of the mid-seventeenth century,

had narrowed and hardened in the people's minds through centuries of repetition.

The chief beliefs of Knox's Calvinism are the absolute power, justice, and holiness of God, and the total sinfulness of man. Man's will was corrupted by the Fall in the Garden of Eden, and he can do nothing to contribute to his own salvation. He deserves eternal damnation. But God in mercy chooses some—the Elect—unconditionally to salvation, and, in justice, condemns others to eternal punishment. Christ died as a substitute for the Elect, taking their just punishment upon himself. Calvary therefore gives God legal justification for sparing them. Their faith and consequently their salvation are bestowed upon them arbitrarily, and do not issue from the moral quality of their lives; personal righteousness is an evidence of salvation, not a cause.

As MacDonald grew into manhood, he increasingly felt that the first purpose of Christian faith was to help people live righteous lives. Christ did not come to declare people righteous before they became so in fact, but rather to enable people to become righteous persons. The Calvinism he saw around him seemed for the most part to make people more concerned with "being right" than with obeying Christ's precepts. He found in the Bible a very different spirit. His convictions were deepened through his diligent Bible reading, especially of the Gospels, and his development of an intimate mystical relationship with God.

He discovered that trying to obey the scriptural precepts with a complete reliance upon the presence of Christ transformed life into a joyous adventure. The person and will of God began to become inexpressibly beautiful, a true satisfaction for his needs and desires. Believing the great truths clearly taught in the Bible was all that was necessary. The more obscure passages, upon which sectarian doctrines were based, should not preoccupy one's attention nor divide Christian from Christian. The more precise shape that MacDonald's beliefs took will be indicated in the chapters that follow. They were rooted in his boyhood experiences, foremost among them being his relationship to his father.

EARLY EDUCATION

Many elements of MacDonald's fiction have their roots in his boyhood attitudes and experiences. These experiences would include his crusading against liquor (MacDonald was at thirteen the first president of the Huntly Juvenile Temperance Society), his fascination for horses, and his love of the sea. Events at school also play a prominent part in his work. The privilege of receiving an education was open to all, the Scottish tradition being one of equality in education. In fact, young George learned his Latin and mathematics sitting beside the sons of "lairds," or landowners. But this privilege was not without its darker side: the discipline in Scottish schools was strict, and incorrect recitations were serious offenses. The inhumane Murdoch Malison, the "dominie" (teacher) in one of MacDonald's better novels, *Alec Forbes of Howglen*, was modeled after his first schoolmaster. When George's eight-year-old brother James died, his schoolmates felt the overly severe discipline administered by this instructor was the chief cause (*GMDW*, 60). A second schoolmaster, decidedly more humane than the first, took kindly to George, occasionally inviting him to his home before and after school hours. Thus encouraged, MacDonald excelled and even helped with the teaching. This teacher no doubt furnishes the model for the many ideal schoolmasters in MacDonald's novels.

CONTACT WITH FAERIE

When MacDonald was sixteen he enrolled in Aulton Grammar School in Aberdeen, some forty miles distant, and there he won a "bursary," or university scholarship, which enabled him to enter King's College. His main course of study there was Chemistry and Natural Philosophy (i.e., Physics), but his desire to become a medical doctor was frustrated by lack of money. Having acquired a working knowledge of German, he became increasingly interested in language and literature, and began writing a considerable amount of poetry. He took his M.A. in April of 1845.

A lack of funds delayed his studies during the 1842–43 school term and he spent his time doing tutorial work. Some early scholars have conjectured that during this hiatus he took a position which involved cataloging a neglected library somewhere in northern Scotland.[3] No

3. See Muriel Hutton, "The George MacDonald Collection," *Yale University Library Gazette*, 51 (1976), 74–85, for an alternate view. In reading MacDonald's letters contained in the Beinecke Rare Book and Manuscript Library at Yale University, Ms. Hutton finds no evidence to support Greville's undocumented assertion of this experience, and therefore questions it, together with certain other details of Greville's account of his father's life. In interesting contrast is Woolf's fantasizing (*GK*, 16–17) that MacDonald fell in love that summer with a girl of the family who owned the library, and was jilted, causing him psychological pain that he tried repeatedly to assuage imaginatively throughout his novel-writing career.

precise records remain of such an experience, but the
many scenes in his novels picturing characters making
spiritual discoveries and having traumatic experiences in
libraries (such as Mr. Cupples in *Alec Forbes* and the narrator in *Lilith)* lead one to suppose that MacDonald
himself faced some spiritual crisis at this time. Greville
quotes a passage from MacDonald's early novel, *The
Portent*, as probably having autobiographical significance:

> Now I was in my element. The very outside of a book
> had a charm to me. It was a kind of sacrament—an
> outward and visible sign of an inward and spiritual
> grace; as, indeed, what on God's earth is not? . . . I
> began to nibble at that portion of the collection which
> belonged to the sixteenth century. . . . I found noth-
> ing, to my idea, but love-poems without any love in
> them, and so I soon became weary. But I found in the
> library what I liked far better—many romances of a
> very marvellous sort, and plentiful interruption they
> gave to the formation of the catalogue. I likewise
> came upon a whole nest of German classics. . . .
> Happening to be a tolerable reader of German, I
> found in these volumes a mine of wealth inex-
> haustible. (*GMDW,* 73)

Two elements are to be noted in this passage. First,
it presents MacDonald's early conviction that God works
on behalf of man through the external world of nature
and event. All things in "God's earth" are a "visible sign
of an inward and spiritual grace." This developing view
suggests a certain departure from a strict Calvinist
understanding of the nature of God and his presence in

the world. MacDonald is beginning to recognize truth as being incarnational rather than strictly propositional.

Second, the above passage suggests MacDonald's enlarging literary interests. Indeed, certain "German classics" began to affect his imagination profoundly, particularly the great German fairy tales. Among them, two works—E. T. A. Hoffmann's *The Golden Pot* and Novalis's *Heinrich von Ofterdingen*—came to have such compelling effect that a direct comparison of them with such early writings as *Phantastes* becomes a profitable study. Such European stories with their special symbolic character enhanced MacDonald's love of his native Scottish land of Faerie and furnished the basic inspiration for his own magnificent fairy tales.

Another influence on MacDonald was the general philosophic position of German Romanticism, which afforded him a specific basis for challenging and modifying some of the tenets of his Calvinist theology. The German Romantics were marked by a tendency to contemplate and idealize man, his emotions, and his position in the cosmos.[4] They were convinced that all things are related and that the universe is characterized by a pervading unity, a unity discoverable to man's reason governed by his intuition. They were much concerned that man's reason be viewed in light of his total being rather than allowed to become his controlling faculty, discrediting the imagination and destroying man's spirit. In addition, they had an appreciation for individuality and a conviction that one's life can have an inner

4. A good source to consult for a discussion of the main traits of German Romanticism is Oskar Walzel, *German Romanticism* (New York: Putnam, 1932).

harmony commensurate with that which they saw in the outer universe. To them, the most important aspect of man's inner being is his yearning after the eternal and the infinite—a type of spiritual love which draws man toward the divine. This love finds its counterpart in the love of man for woman, so that passionate love mirrors spiritual love. Lastly, they were convinced that poetry is absolute reality, ultimate truth, knowledge itself. Such outspoken claims for verbal art are found most specifically in Novalis's thought, with which MacDonald identified strongly. His own claims for the moral and spiritual efficacy of the spirit of poetry and song are expressed in such works as *Phantastes* and *At the Back of the North Wind.*

During this break from his university studies, MacDonald's imagination was growing and his own religious views were being modified. What begins to emerge is a dynamic synthesis of orthodox Calvinism and German Romanticism.

PORTRAIT OF THE COLLEGE STUDENT

MacDonald in his college days was a rather dreamy—but on occasions fiery—young Celt. He was a debater, an enthusiast of the then popular parlor game of charades, and a lover of beautiful clothes, being especially fond of his Scottish tartan coat. Somewhat aloof and reserved, he gave the general impression of being a thoughtful youth whose full powers were yet to be realized. Physically he was never strong—he suffered periods throughout his life of bronchitis, asthma, and what may have been tuberculosis. But his active mind was forming a faith that would accommodate his enlarging views of life and those of the German authors he was reading.

He was writing poetry for his own solace during his college days, and one source of poetic inspiration for him was an attractive and talented cousin, Helen MacKay, some three years his senior. They had been childhood playmates, and they conducted a correspondence in later years, but she was of most help to him at this time, encouraging his literary pursuits. When Greville was collecting data for his book, the aged Helen recalled "a favorite saying of his then was, 'I wis we war a' deid!' and that he often repeated it in after life." (*GMDW*, 64.) MacDonald's fascination with death should be understood in terms of his positive trust in a loving God. The biblical promise of eternal life for faithful followers of Christ prompted his anticipation of its glorious realization. A Christian's death is birth into fuller life. This attitude is present throughout his writings, culminating in *Lilith*. It most assuredly does not indicate a morbid depression of spirit, bitterness, or a rejection of this life.[5]

MARRIAGE

Upon leaving King's College, MacDonald took a tutorship in Fulham, a parish in London, and during this period he began to court Louisa Powell, sister-in-law to

5. Woolf accepts MacDonald's use of this expression as certain evidence that he was deeply "mournful and depressed" during this period (*GK*, 17). That he was preoccupied with death is also evident from the poem "Love Me, Beloved," which he presented to his wife on their wedding day, and which Woolf quotes in support of his contention (*GK*, 20–22). Still, these somber expressions do not prove that MacDonald was mentally unhealthy. His fascination for death, with the expectation of ecstatic experience beyond, was more probably being fed by Novalis's attitudes on the subject, found throughout his writings.

the now-married Helen MacKay. She was the dutiful but light-hearted daughter of a stern Puritan whose family business was in the leather trade. His experience in teaching having proved disappointing, MacDonald now began to prepare for the ministry, a step which he had been contemplating for some time, and entered Highbury Theological College in London in 1848. His university training enabled him to complete the four-year course in two years, and he was soon doing apprentice preaching. After Mr. Powell was satisfied that MacDonald had a future as a Congregational minister, he consented to the marriage and the wedding took place on March 8, 1851. The couple settled at Arundel, in West Sussex, where MacDonald had his first charge as pastor of the Trinity Congregational Church.

THE HETERODOX PASTOR

Many in the congregation at Arundel were soon disquieted with the sermons of their new pastor. MacDonald's emphasis upon obeying Christ's teachings in everyday life seemed quite removed from the expositions of Calvinist doctrines which they wanted to hear. His experiences as a pastor, however, only served to strengthen his convictions. His letters, together with autobiographical remarks in his novels, show much about how his beliefs were forming.

MacDonald writes in his novel *Weighed and Wanting* many years later: "I well remember . . . feeling as a child that I did not care for God to love me if he did not love everybody: the kind of love I needed was the love that all men needed, the love that belonged to their nature as the children of the Father, a love he could not give me except he gave it to all men." This passage suggests that as a boy he must have been at least uneasy about the doctrines of limited atonement and unconditional election. With a disposition that could not long maintain a negative approach, he began to feel that God was, as Creator, everyone's Father, and that His mercy extended impartially to all. Excerpts from two letters that Greville provides from the period of his father's tutorship show his state of mind prior to his pastorship:

MacDonald to his Father

One of my greatest difficulties in consenting to think of religion was that I thought I should have to give up my beautiful things and my love for the things God had made. But I find that the happiness springing from all things not in themselves sinful is much increased by religion. God is the God of the beautiful, Religion the love of the Beautiful, and Heaven the home of the Beautiful, Nature is tenfold brighter in the sun of Righteousness, and my love of Nature is more intense since I became a Christian—if indeed I am one. God has not given me such things and forbidden me to enjoy them. . . .

MacDonald to his Uncle

I called on Dr. Adams, but had again the misfortune to find that he was out. I do not think I am right to use the word misfortune, for the conviction is, I think, growing on me that the smallest events are ordered

for us, while yet in perfect consistency with the
ordinary course of cause and effect in the world. I
am strongly inclined to think that whatever has a
moral effect of any kind on our minds, God manages
far us. . . . (*GMDW,* 108–109)

One quickly notes how some of his most deeply held
convictions are emerging. God is the joyous Creator of a
beautiful world, and He intends for man to enjoy it. God
is behind not only the good and the beautiful in the
world, but the so-called "misfortunes" as well, creating an
ultimate good for all His children.

Similarly positive are MacDonald's letters to his
fiancee, which go beyond mere lover's rhetoric in considering the nature of love, linking it with the life of God:

Is love a beautiful thing, dearest? You and I love: but
who created love? Let us ask him to purify our love to
make it stronger and more real and more self-denying.
I want to love you for ever—so that, though there is
not marrying or giving in marriage in heaven, we may
see each other there as the best beloved. Oh Louisa, is
it not true that our life here is a growing unto life, and
our death a being born—our true birth? If there is anything beautiful in this our dreamy life, shall it not
shine forth in glory in the bright waking consciousness
of heaven? . . . But . . . we can only expect to be a bless-
ing to each other—by doing that which is right. . . .
(*GMDW,* 117)

In his writings MacDonald both idealizes woman and
also views her as more equal to man than did the typical
Victorian male. The loving partnership of marriage is

one of God's most primary expressions of grace. It teaches both partners more of what love is, it grows in the context of upright living, and it issues in the individual spiritual maturing of both partners. Beneath the sentimentality, MacDonald is expressing a genuine sensitivity to the true nature of love.[6]

These ideas, however, were far out of keeping with what his Congregationalist parishioners then wanted to hear. Further, when MacDonald in 1851 published his translations, "Twelve of the Spiritual Songs of Novalis," they rejected him saying he was tainted by German thought.[7] When MacDonald expressed from the pulpit his hope that animals would have a share in the joys of heaven, and that the opportunity for the heathen to be saved did not end at their death, the congregation was aroused to indignant action. They drastically reduced his salary in the hope he would thereby be forced to resign. Never reluctant to accept poverty if such were God's will, MacDonald simply responded that he and his family would live on less. But when he saw that his staying was encouraging a schism, he resigned in 1853.

FREELANCE PREACHER AND LECTURER

A period of great hardship and disappointment followed. Poverty-stricken, MacDonald took his family to the industrial metropolis of Manchester and rented a room on Renshaw Street, preaching regularly for those who would listen, and expressing freely his growing

---

6. Cf. MacDonald's discussion of love in his essay "Individual Development," *ADO*, 43–76.

7. ". . . he was emboldened to print in Arundel his translations . . . for private circulation as a Christmas gift to his friends" (*GMDW*, 159).

convictions. He was especially attracted to Manchester because of the presence there of Alexander John Scott, Principal of Owens College, a man he greatly admired. Later, he dedicated his novel *Robert Falconer* to him. In Manchester MacDonald began his lecturing career by advertising lessons on English literature, the physical sciences, and theology. Those who attended paid a modest sum. Such efforts were difficult because he was fighting tuberculosis and attacks of bronchitis at the time, but he was the more burdened because he and Louisa were constantly dependent on their families, the Powells and the MacDonalds, together with contributions from a few admirers, for their support.[8] MacDonald's father tried to be sympathetic to his son during this period, though he advised him in one letter to "give over the fruitless game of poetry, and apply yourself to the preaching of the Gospel." MacDonald's sorrow was deepened by two deaths in his family: his brother John died of tuberculosis in 1858, and his father died suddenly a month later. His father's death was a great blow to him because of the deep emotional bond.

THE YOUNG FATHER

In spite of the adulatory tone that Greville maintains throughout his biography, in his later *Reminiscences of a*

8. Greville gives this picture of family conditions at his birth: "When at last I arrived on a foggy winter's day in 1856, my father, then lying at the house of his friend, Alexander J. Scott, principal of Owens College, Manchester, seemed to be dying of haemorrhage from the lungs. Yet in spite of scribbling forbidden notes to my mother to reciprocate her joy that a boy was now added to their three little girls, the danger was arrested. Within a fortnight my mother was preparing to leave a city that offered small chance of his cure. For two years he had by teaching subsisted precariously, heroic alike in industry and ailing,

Specialist he depicts a somewhat more human father. For instance, he remarks, ". . . my father, I think, did not altogether understand children, though in his books he so fully realized their needs," and he records the following:

> When I was nine, my father gave me a box of tools, and a little bench with an adorable vice that squeaked vilely but never held. They gave me infinite happiness. . . . One recompense was an admonishment from my father over an attempt at box-making; and I have never forgotten it: "If ever you do anything badly and content yourself with saying, 'Oh, that'll have to do!' then you may be sure it won't do at all!" It represented well a stoic quality in his own creed: "God," he once said, "is not hard to please, but it is impossible to satisfy Him.". . . My father began to teach me Latin when I was nine, I think. The initial lesson dealt with the opening lines of the Aeneid. He first translated them, and tried to make me feel their metric thrill; then I had to commit them to my impossible memory. But I did not understand him; and the words had no more meaning than if he had himself invented them just for a lesson. Such a system might be good for a clever boy; but it was worse than useless for me. For it suggested that foreign words were hateful and meant only *tasks*. He failed almost as much with Euclid. I recall his patient attempts to explain, with the help of matches, the first of the Axioms; and how, hypnotized by my own wrong version, even punishment failed to help me. At last the *pons*

while my mother tended and taught her children, . . . kept the house and its furniture spotless, yet always the lover and support of her husband . . ." (*ROS*, 12, 13). Greville's praise of his mother is consistently strong.

asinorum, easily traversed by a sister, proved me hopeless. And there the lessons ceased. Yet later at school I was singularly facile with geometry. [9]

MacDonald was his own taskmaster, and evidently this stern attitude, coupled with high expectations for both intellectual endeavor and moral conduct, shaped his family life as well as his writings. On the one hand, he held a vision of mercy and patience of widest compass; on the other, he felt intensely that children were responsible to follow goodness with dedication of spirit and to be diligent in realizing their highest ethical and intellectual potential. In retrospect, Greville apparently entertained some reservations about how his father implemented these convictions.

EARLY WRITINGS

The 1850's mark the beginning of MacDonald's career as a writer. In addition to sustaining throughout his life steady preaching engagements and regular lecture tours, he produced, with amazing energy, over fifty published volumes of fantasy, poetry, novels, fairy tales and young people's stories, sermons, essays, translations of German authors, and literary criticism.[10] This study is concerned primarily with his fantasies, but it is important to consider his poems and novels as well.

MacDonald's initial success came in 1855 with the publication of *Within and Without,* an extended poem

9. *ROS,* 15, 31.
10. Two studies of MacDonald's literary work are Richard Reis, *George MacDonald's Fiction* (1972; Eureka, Calif: Sunrise, 1989) and David S. Rob, *God's Fiction: Symbolism and Allegory in the Works of George MacDonald* (1987; Eureka,Calif: Sunrise, 1989).

that melodramatically details the experiences of an aspiring monk who escapes the monastery, marries, and comes through many difficult experiences into a true relation with God. This was followed in 1857 by a second small volume of poems, the most noted of which is "The Hidden Life." He discovered his true literary strength in 1858, however, with *Phantastes: A Faerie Romance for Men and Women.* It is a fantasy in which MacDonald presents the hero as discovering moral and spiritual truths in a rapidly occurring series of highly symbolic adventures in Faerie. More attention will be given to his rich symbolism in later chapters.

MacDonald was disturbed with a certain reviewer's attempt to call *Phantastes* allegory, insisting that if a reader find some truths behind its symbolism, well and good, but it was to be read simply for the joy of the story. The story exhibits the author's ability, found as well in the later children's fairy tales and *Lilith*, to invest the fairy world with a startling reality while at the same time retaining its atmosphere of magic and wonder. Sadly, however, it was not well received by contemporary readers. Critics ridiculed it and few copies sold.

LITERARY FRIENDS AND INFLUENCES

MacDonald's budding writing career enabled him to become acquainted with many prominent Victorian authors. Among the most interesting of his close friendships was one with Lady Byron, the poet's widow, who admired MacDonald so profoundly that from 1855 until her death in 1860 she became the MacDonald family's

steady benefactor.[11] Because of his poor health, she
sponsored the family for a winter in Algiers in 1856–57,
and in her will she left them 300 pounds. It was at her
home that Henry Crabb Robinson, the famous diarist,
met MacDonald in April of 1859. He describes
MacDonald as "a very interesting man . . . an invalid
and a German scholar. . . . His connections are among
the Dissenters . . . yet [he] is quite liberal."[12] Lady Byron
was also responsible for introducing MacDonald to
several others in the literary circles of the time, such as
Frederick Denison Maurice, Charles Kingsley, Matthew
Arnold, and John Ruskin.

Very little information exists on the exact nature of
these friendships. Greville writes: "My father and mother, what with his ill-health and the demands of the young
family upon herself, together with their poverty, could
not move much in the social world. Yet . . . Charles
Kingsley, Matthew Arnold, and Henry Crabb Robinson
ranked among their intimates, even if they did not meet
very often . . ." (*GMDW,* 300). One gets the feeling that
the MacDonalds were on the periphery of the social life
of their time, maintaining certain warm ties with those
who admired MacDonald's thought and abilities, but
placing higher value on such things as family life and
MacDonald's ministry rather than on social activity as
such. Those friends who were closest to them are

11. This patronage gives interesting insight into Lady Byron's character:
MacDonald stood considerably nearer her ideal than did her late husband. She
is fictionalized as Lady Bernard in *The Vicar's Daughter*—a most flattering
portrait.

12. Edith J. Morley, ed., *Henry Crabb Robinson on Books and Their Writers,* ii
(London: Dent, 1938), 783. A friend of a large number of nineteenth-century
authors, Robinson left much information about them in his diary and his correspondence.

described by Greville as being almost a part of the MacDonald family.

Perhaps the closest family friend was Charles L. Dodgson (Lewis Carroll), who, Greville writes, was "especially intimate in our home, as in our hearts" (*GMDW*, 301). He calls him "Uncle Dodgson," and recalls how the manuscript of *Alice in Wonderland* was first submitted to MacDonald for his evaluation ("illustrated with pen-and-ink sketches and minutely penned in printing characters" (*GMDW*, 342). MacDonald suggested it be read to his children for their reactions, and as a result of their lively enthusiasm it was published. This friendship is understandable because the two men shared a love of children and an especial ability to recreate imaginatively a children's world.

With two of the more prominent literati listed above, Arnold and Ruskin, MacDonald shared a vivid sense of moral urgency. Although Arnold and Ruskin stand rather far from MacDonald's religious commitment, MacDonald consistently placed the necessity of adhering to high moral concepts above any sectarian agreement on the dogmatic doctrinal basis for these concepts, and, unlike most Evangelicals, he could find an enriching fellowship with men of differing doctrinal persuasions. He did share common ground with both men: Arnold celebrated Wordsworth, whom MacDonald greatly admired for, among other qualities, the strength of his moral vision and his application of moral ideas to life, and Ruskin built a careful argument for a moral aesthetic.[13] In

13. See Arnold's poem "Memorial Verses" for his general tribute and his article on Wordsworth for his specific emphasis upon Wordsworth's morality; see MacDonald's essay "Wordsworth's Poetry," *ADO*, 245–263, for his assessment of Wordsworth. Ruskin outlines his moral aesthetic in *Modern Painters*.

addition, MacDonald acted as a confidante to Ruskin during his tumultuous love affair with Rose La Touche, an episode about which Greville includes much interesting material (*GMDW,* 328ff.).

The friends who did most to influence the direction of MacDonald's theological thinking during this time were the aforementioned Alexander John Scott and Frederick Denison Maurice. Little can be said about the precise religious position of Scott, since he left no important writings. His orthodoxy had also been questioned—he was disfranchised from the Presbyterian ministry for preaching universalism—and thus he was able to encourage and counsel sympathetically the rejected minister from Arundel at the crucial time of his moving to Manchester. But the most prominent Victorian theologian to influence MacDonald's thought was Maurice. He was an ambivalent figure who, like MacDonald, tended to be too liberal for the conservatives and too conservative for the liberals. He was ahead of his time, a High Churchman with a social conscience—he coined the phrase "Christian Socialism" and was the leader of that movement in the 1840's. Throughout his career as educator and minister he published widely. He was a Trinitarian but was more Unitarian than Evangelical. Most Evangelical formulations of doctrine appeared too crass and materialistic to him, and he repeatedly attempted a more profoundly spiritual interpretation of the biblical "proof texts" used by Evangelicals to establish these positions. A man whose deep practical spirituality lent a moral beauty to his life, Maurice was ecumenical in spirit, feeling that there was some truth in all religious experience, Christian and otherwise.

MacDonald became a disciple of his in the late 1850's. Among the ideas that MacDonald clearly shared with him were his stress upon the Fatherhood of God and the conviction that Christ is absolutely at one with the Father (a doctrine that renders impossible any view of the Atonement as bringing about a change in God's attitude toward man—forgiveness was God's disposition from eternity past). Both rejected the idea that sin would be eternally punished, emphasized the "Inner Light" with the possibility of revelation to the individual apart from Scripture (but not inharmonious with it), and insisted that theology undergirds all of life, all branches of knowledge being subservient to it.

Within the Christian Socialist movement being shaped by Maurice, Charles Kingsley was a prominent novelist. Although MacDonald was not actively a part of this movement, he shared Kingsley's concern for the social and religious problems of the laboring people.[14] MacDonald's novels *Robert Falconer* and *Guild Court* manifest this type of social concern. *The Water Babies*, Kingsley's moralizing fairy story published in 1863, also bears a resemblance, perhaps derivative, to MacDonald's *Phantastes* (1858).

---

14. Joseph Ellis Baker, *The Novel and the Oxford Movement* (Princeton: Princeton University Press, 1932). Though old, this is a useful study of how the novel was at this time used for religious purposes. Baker discusses a number of minor religious novelists. So also does Robert Lee Woolf in *Gains and Losses: Novels of Faith and Doubt in Victorian England* (New York: Garland, 1977). Woolf is good for plot summaries.

THE TURN TO THE NOVEL

The popular success of such propagandist novelists as
Charles Kingsley, who was advocating social reforms,
encouraged MacDonald to try his hand at writing novels.
No doubt his decision to attempt realistic stories was also
influenced by the failure of *Phantastes*. If the public could
not appreciate his symbolic vision, he had to express
himself more directly. Greville remarks on his father's
"conviction that the world was so sorely in need of his
message" (*GMDW,* 324). His ministry to the people of his
day was his primary motivation, but the need for money
to support his growing family was, of course, also a factor. Perhaps his pen could be made to pay.

His publisher friend George Murray Smith urged
him: ". . . if you would but write novels, you would find
all the publishers saving up to buy them of you! Nothing
but fiction pays" (*GMDW,* 318). The result was that he
turned from fantasy to the novel in order to communicate
his convictions to the world.

MacDonald possessed the unmistakable gift of telling a
story with compelling power and narrative grace, and he
understood clearly the art of novel writing. Nevertheless,
his early attempts at novels were too weighted with
preaching for any publisher to accept.[15] Then a remark-
able exception, *The Portent,* appeared in *Cornhill
Magazine,* summer issue, in 1860. This short novel is free
from direct teaching; its plot turns upon the fact that
some of the characters possess Celtic second sight. When

15. After publishing *Phantastes,* MacDonald wrote a play entitled *If I Had a
Father,* which he then turned into a novel entitled *Seekers and Finders.* He failed
to secure a publisher for the novel, and finally published the play with some
fairy stories in *The Gifts of the Christ Child and Other Tales* in 1882.

his wife pressed him for its meaning, MacDonald somewhat embarrassedly confessed that he simply "wrote it
for the tale" (*GMDW,* 318).

In his dedicatory preface to *The Portent,* MacDonald
observes that a novel must offer insight into human
nature and experience, and it must do so in a form characterized by a "harmony within," or inner consistency.
These simple but telling artistic standards go far in measuring the art of MacDonald's subsequent novels, their
strengths and weaknesses.

His first published novel was *David Elginbrod* (1863),
which, although it somewhat relieved his financial
distress, contained sufficient heterodoxy to prevent him
from receiving the Chair of Rhetoric and Belles Lettres
at Edinburgh University for which he applied in 1865.
The kernel idea for the story came to MacDonald at a
business dinner for literary celebrities. He was deeply
affected by hearing a journalist recite an old Scotch
epitaph:

> Here lie I, Martin Elginbrodde;
> Hae mercy o' my soul, Lord God;
> As I wad do, were I Lord God,
> An'ye war Martin Elginbrodde!

This verse must have suggested to MacDonald man's
need for God's mercy, and the essential unity between the
divine and the human, ideas which are important in all
his writings. *David Elginbrod,* whose hero is modeled
after MacDonald's father, was flatteringly received by the
critics, and met with moderate success. It was even translated into German in 1873.

MacDonald apparently was not satisfied with the prospect of writing only realistic novels. He wanted to try again to make his readers understand symbolic tales. The following year, 1864, marks the appearance of *Adela Cathcart*, a work that attempts to bring together fantasy and realism. In it a framework of realistic narrative contains a number of experiments in symbolic tales, from fairy story through various moral anecdotes to parable. But the experiment was not well received, which evidently made MacDonald determined to keep the two genres more distinctly separate. His own dissatisfaction is registered in the thorough reworking that he gave the material for a second edition in 1882, omitting from it three of his better stories—"The Light Princess," "The Shadows," and "The Giant's Heart"—and reprinting them elsewhere as children's stories.

Reverting to realism, he produced in the following two years two ambitious novels, *Alec Forbes of Howglen* and *Annals of a Quiet Neighbourhood*. The former is a remarkably vivid tale of an orphan girl and Alec Forbes, which traces their growing up together, both physically and spiritually, and their eventual love. The latter book, narrated by a young pastor, depicts his experiences in a small-town parish—experiences based upon MacDonald's life in Arundel. With his name now established as an important young novelist, MacDonald began to rapidly produce novels which expressed his interpretation of life. They fall into two general categories, the Scottish and the English. The first of the former is *David Elginbrod*, with its initial Scottish setting and its studied attempt to reproduce the Scottish dialect; the second is *Alec Forbes of Howglen*. In the category of English novels, the first is

Adela Cathcart, with its framework of thoroughly English setting and customs, and *Annals of a Quiet Neighbourhood* is, if *The Portent* is discounted because of its shortness, the second.

Over the next thirty years he produced more than twenty novels, in addition to the above titles, that blend realism and romance. The works can be divided into the two ethnic categories defined (though there is, of course, some overlapping). In the English group, chronological-ly, fall the following titles: *Guild Court* (1868), *The Seaboard Parish* (1868), *The Vicar's Daughter* (1872), *Wilfrid Cumbermede* (1872), *Thomas Wingfold, Curate* (1876), *Paul Faber, Surgeon* (1879), *Mary Marston* (1881), *Weighed and Wanting* (1882), *What's Mine's Mine* (1886), *Home Again* (1887), and *There and Back* (1891). The remaining titles in the Scottish group are *Robert Falconer* (1868), *Malcolm* (1875), *The Marquis of Lossie* (1877), *Sir Gibbie* (1879), *Warlock O'Glenwarlock* (1882), *Donal Grant* (1883), *The Elect Lady* (1888), *A Rough Shaking* (1890), *The Flight of the Shadow* (1891), *Heather and Snow* (1893), and *Salted with Fire* (1897). One historical novel, *St. George and St. Michael* (1876), set during the Puritan Revolution, is par-ticularly interesting for its sympathetic treatment of the English Catholics.

Viewing all the novels as a body, one notes little change either in technique or in underlying ideas. A few of his works, such as *The Elect Lady* and *The Flight of the Shadow,* are obviously too quickly written and of inferior quality. It is also true that one finds stock incidents and characters in all of the novels. Nevertheless, MacDonald's love of life and his psychological insights, together with his keen ability to reproduce Scottish dialect and the flavor of Scottish attitudes, result in many delightful portions, particularly in the Scottish group. And his epigrammatic turn of phrase coupled with his exacting insights into experience often gives memorable expression to basic moral and spiritual ideas, many of which could hardly be denied, even by the most unsympathetic reader.

CHILDREN'S LITERATURE

MacDonald also stands as one of the century's finest authors of children's literature. In 1869 he accepted the editorship of a periodical for children entitled *Good Words for the Young*. It lasted for only four years, and during the final two years MacDonald edited the periodical without pay. He was fortunate to have some of his own fairy stories first published in it, although the ill feelings of those whose manuscripts were refused made him determine that he would do no more editing at any salary. But his love of the children's story and fairy tale continued throughout his lifetime, and most of his titles are still found in the children's rooms of public libraries. His fairy tales were published separately, and have appeared in many different editions down to the present time.

Among his children's books the most widely read are *At the Back of the North Wind* (1871), *The Princess and the Goblin* (1872), and *The Princess and Curdie* (1883), each of which contains genuine charm. (Each of the fantasies will be examined in later chapters.) MacDonald's great strength in each is the manner in which he makes the supernatural seem immediately real. Two full-length novels, *Ranald Bannerman's Boyhood* (1871) and *Gutta Percha Willie: The Working Genius* (1873), fall somewhere between the children's stories and the adult fiction, and may most properly be classified as adolescent novels.

LECTURES AND FAMILY AFFAIRS

In addition to his ambitious career as a writer, MacDonald found time for other noteworthy concerns. For a time he was a lecturer at evening classes at King's College, London. (His own university conferred upon him the degree of Doctor of Laws in 1868.) He spent the winter of 1872–73 on a lecture tour of America, in which he visited cities throughout the East and went as far west as St. Louis.[16] As a platform speaker he was very well received, his lectures on Robert Burns being the most popular. During the tour he met the literary great, among them the poet John Greenleaf Whittier and, remarkably, Mark Twain, who later returned the visit to England.

MacDonald's private life was also full. Problems of health prompted his decision to have the family winter regularly in Italy, and in 1891 he planned and built his own home in Bordighera on the Italian Riviera, naming it Casa Coraggio, a large dwelling built on the strength of a generous purse raised by several wealthy admirers. Together with his eleven children, their home now accommodated several foster children, frequent visitors, and, from time to time, various needy people whom the MacDonalds undertook to help get back on their feet. The oldest daughter, Lilia, possessed an extraordinary talent for acting, and, although her parents would not

16. See Greville, *ROS*, 47–52, for his glowing account of MacDonald's reception in America.

allow her to become an actress on the secular stage, for
years the family project for each summer was to return to
England as a family acting troupe, presenting dramas in
public halls and private homes. In their repertoire were
Macbeth, a version of Zola's *L'Assommoir*, some of
Dickens, and many of MacDonald's fairy tales. (The
adaptations of the texts for the stage were largely the
work of Louisa, MacDonald's wife.) Their most popular
presentation was a rendition of *Pilgrim's Progress;* Lilia
became quite well-known as Christiana and MacDonald
himself played Mr. Greatheart, the other parts being
carried by the other members of the family. On Sunday
and Wednesday afternoons Casa Coraggio was open to
the public, and MacDonald regularly presented devotional discourses and lectures on Dante and on English
literature, focusing particularly on Shakespeare.

The activities of these later years, however, were
marred by increasing problems of health and the toll of
tuberculosis upon the family. Tuberculosis claimed
MacDonald's daughter Mary Josephine, engaged to a
talented young artist, in 1878; a delicate-natured son in
1879; a recently married daughter in 1884; and the highly
talented Lilia in 1891. These heartaches put strong
demands upon the solace that his anagram— "Corage!
God Mend Al!"—offered.

One noteworthy literary result of the severe trials of
MacDonald's life is *A Book of Strife, in the Form of the
Diary of an Old Soul* (1880), a devotional poem of 366
stanzas, one for each day of the year (including the
"extra" day of a leap year). John Ruskin described it as
"quaint, full of devotion, high in tone, the best example

of the survival of faith in this sceptical age" (*GMDW*, 497). Its sentiments are at times strongly mystical and esoteric; nevertheless, MacDonald's sensitive and intimate presentation of the devout soul's various feelings before God make this a poem of great devotional value.

MacDonald expressed his convictions in expository form in *The Miracles Of our Lord* (1870), three volumes entitled *Unspoken Sermons* (1867, 1886, and 1889), and *The Hope of the Gospel* (1892).[17] He distrusted all abstract systems of thought, and he avoided systematizing his own, but his convictions are thoroughly consistent with each other, and quite comprehensive theologically. He is sensitive to the shortcomings of language and metaphor in presenting divine realities, and he tends to see all doctrinal formulations as being but sets of opinions. He has, on the other hand, an intense reverence for the text of Scripture, and he speaks compellingly out of careful and profound meditations upon selected Scripture passages, frequently showing a deft ability to handle the Greek text. He is insistent upon the necessity of Christians thinking carefully and consistently upon all of Scripture, and he does not avoid texts that on the surface would appear to negate some of his own positions. He does not hesitate to show his righteous indignation toward what he perceived to be the spiritual crassness and intellectual shortsightedness of many in the Christian community of his day. Invariably, his emphasis falls upon the vital importance of a childlike obedience to scriptural precepts. All those who are interested in his

17. References to individual sermons will hereafter be by their titles, together with the following abbreviations: *US I* (London, 1867); *US II* (London, 1886); *US III* (London, 1889); and *HG* for *The Hope of the Gospel* (London, 1892).

thought should directly consult these sermons and theological essays.

MacDonald's full and varied career came to its close in the 1890s. As an aged man, he aspired to compose a final, crowning fictional statement of his body of convictions, and the result was a second fantasy for adults, entitled *Lilith* (1895). The penetrating logic of its controlling ideas and the haunting reality of its dream imagery make it an outstanding example of mythopoeia, worthy of careful reading. He died at Ashtead, Surrey, on September 18, 1905; his body was cremated, and his ashes buried at Bordighera.

CONCLUSION

George MacDonald tried earnestly to humanize his Calvinist theological inheritance, both directly, through theological essays, and indirectly, through novels, fantasies, and children's fairy tales. On the theological and literary scenes, he stood somewhat apart from his contemporaries. With characteristic humility, he avoided engaging others in controversy or criticizing his contemporaries by name. He was a poet and novelist, not a controversialist, and he was devoted to reaching as many people as he could with his vision of the true nature of life. He dedicated his artistic talents to helping people who were alienated from contemporary Christianity because it presented a God too small in his purposes and concerns and a view of life that was unrealistic and distorted. He felt his art could show that a true faith became joyous as it discovered that fully following Christ turned everyday life into an exciting adventure. Writing novels gave him the opportunity to lay bare the very core of human nature and experience, where he saw his principles confirmed. There was a God-shaped vacuum in every human heart.

MacDonald was not a thinker concerned only with internal matters in Evangelicalism, unaware or unheeding of the great issues that confronted the church in his day. He deplored the encroachments of the mechanistic approach of science upon any of the sundry aspects of life. He hated any expression of materialism as well, and treated with keen irony anyone who felt that money was the answer to one's ills. Certainly he did not think that money should be despised, but rather that it should be viewed as sacred—a means to possible good. The tendency of the period to associate material progress with spiritual values, looking upon riches as a proper reward for work combined with the proper virtues, was to him contemptible.

He was undisturbed by certain contemporary ideas that influenced some other authors to alter greatly or reject completely their orthodox Christian heritage. The rise of evolutionary theory, which many Evangelicals saw as devastating to their faith, was something MacDonald welcomed. Like Robert Browning, he saw it as lending strong support to his doctrine of individual spiritual development and growth, and it reinforced his optimism for the moral future of mankind. Another source of attack on Christian faith, German Higher Criticism of the biblical text, left many intellectuals of the period spiritually bereft, but it disturbed MacDonald little. He was not perturbed chiefly because he felt the raw intellect simply was unable to comprehend Christianity apart from the response of full obedience. The purpose of the written word was to enable the reader to meet the Living Word, Christ. He has little to say about Higher Criticism in his writings, but an essay in *Orts* on Browning's "Christmas Eve" shows his full agreement with that poet's ironic handling of the Gottingen professor who epitomizes for Browning the German rationalist approach to Christianity. The nineteenth-century movements toward social reform received his full sympathy, apparent in his books like *Robert Falconer,* in which the selfless hero helps the poor slum dwellers.

One must observe, however, that MacDonald's theology stops appreciably short of nineteenth-century liberalism. He had a strong vision of personal evil and the necessity of purgation from it, and hence had a clear vision of the consuming fires of God's holiness. The righteousness he championed differs from that of the liberal in that he insisted it is not self-generated; it is produced rather by the presence of Christ within the believer. Nor does righteousness earn salvation, being a product of God's indwelling energies. His emphasis upon subjective experience was not at the expense of the objective reality of God. To MacDonald, man is subsumed in that reality; to the liberal, God is subsumed within the ego. MacDonald's doctrines of the subjugation of the self and of personal immortality also make him distinct from his liberal friends.

MacDonald's convictions have, then, abundant expression in various literary types: sermons, poems, novels, and fantasies. This book will focus greatest attention upon the fantasies and fairy tales for two reasons: first, because his achievement reaches its highest level in this mythopoeic art; and second, because the difficult symbolism of the fantasies may be illumined by carefully noting what specific convictions helped to shape his art. In *The Princess and the Goblin* and *The Princess and Curdie* a basic theme is that salvation is in its very nature the experience of growing in righteousness.

Chapter 2

Glowing, Flaming Roses, Red and White

"I was doing the wrong of never wanting
or trying to be better."

—Curdie in *The Princess and Curdie*

In one of the initial meetings between the mystical old queen Irene and Curdie in *The Princess and Curdie*, the queen explains to him about spiritual growth and retrogression:

"Have you ever heard what some philosophers say—
that men were all animals once?"

"No, ma'am."

"It is of no consequence. But there is another
thing that is of the greatest consequence—this: that
all men, if they do not take care, go down hill to the
animals' country; that many men are actually, all their

lives, going to be beasts. People knew it once, but it is long since they forgot it."

"I am not surprised to hear it, ma'am, when I think of some of our miners."

"Ah! But you must beware, Curdie, how you say of this man or that man that he is travelling beast-ward. There are not nearly so many going that way as at first sight you might think. When you met your father on the hill tonight, you stood and spoke together on the same spot; and although one of you was going up and the other coming down, at a little distance no one could have told which was bound in the one direction and which in the other. Just so two people may be at the same spot in manners and behavior, and yet one may be getting better and the other worse, which is just the greatest of all differences that could possibly exist between them.

Here is a concept that appears in almost all of MacDonald's stories. It may be called his doctrine of becoming.[1] Much of the symbolism of *The Princess and the Goblin* and *The Princess and Curdie* gives imaginative expression to this idea.

MacDonald believed it was possible for mankind to grow into complete godlikeness, so that people could be

1. Woolf speaks of MacDonald's "concept of two-way evolution" (*GK*, 167), and curiously remarks about "hideous beasts, like Lina," that "those on the way up are better than those on the way down, a profoundly depressing way of saying that animals are really better than human beings" (*GK*, 177). Reis uses the term "spiritual education" to discuss MacDonald's concept of "man's life as a step-wise progress of cumulative enlightenment" (125). The essential consideration is the strength of MacDonald's emphasis on the spiritual aspect of man. MacDonald is saying people grow or diminish in the very spiritual quality of their beings, and that a certain quality of being is prerequisite to the under-standing of any spiritual truth. The more one grows into spiritual maturity, the more truths he is able to receive.

one with God. This does not mean that people shall be absorbed into God, as more pantheistic systems hold; rather, as humans mature into moral and spiritual perfection, they develop at the same time a more distinct individuality. When they shall become full sons of God, each one willing the right and doing the good as naturally as God Himself does, then they will participate in the blessed fellowship that has always existed between God the Father and Christ the Son. MacDonald's vision is one of an innumerable multitude of redeemed individuals with a final unity of will and spirit.

This spiritual evolution is slow because of the mysterious antagonism of the human will to His loving purpose. The tendency is to "go down hill to the animals' country," as the old queen above says. In His working, God does not force Himself upon people, violating their wills; in so doing He would render them something less than human. On the contrary, God, who is unfathomable Love, and who already has loved humankind into being by creating them, envelopes them with His influences, purposing their growth into higher conditions of life. But in this particular earthly life only some respond. And their growth into greater life is not easy; it may be painful because it requires their being purged from all that is antagonistic to God within them.

God is the source and fountainhead of all life, and all of history is the story of God's "divine agony to give divine life" to His creatures. When men imagine themselves weary of life, it is in truth death—or apartness from God—that they are weary of. God's task is to arouse people to choose the life that is in Him, and His working in creation and in history is all to this end. Christ came that people "may have life, and have it abundantly" (John 10:10).

As *The Princess and the Goblin* and *The Princess and Curdie* illustrate, an individual is imperfect and spiritually ignorant according to how far he stands from the fullness of life into which he can grow. In the symbolism of the fantasy, life retrogressing from God may be reborn in another life as animal. But all that happens to the rebellious soul is calculated to effect its eventual repentance and turning toward God. Evil will continue to plague man and hideously distort his spirit until the turning occurs. One day the retrogressing soul may come to see itself as it truly is in God's sight, and, having come to the end of itself, will turn toward God. The experience of Lilith, portrayed in MacDonald's fantasy by that name, is a prime illustration of the soul turning to God after experiencing all the horribly disintegrating effects of sin and self-centeredness. She then begins the process of becoming spiritually whole by dying into life and learning righteousness.

MacDonald often uses Christ's parable of the prodigal son to illustrate this concept. It is to him the central parable of Christianity, offering the basic pattern of spiritual experience for all people. Eternal Love will not be defeated, nor its energies finally wasted. Curdie's Lina, the grotesque but devoted animal that serves him so well in *The Princess and Curdie*, is one of MacDonald's prodigals: she is a soul that, having retrogressed, has now turned and begun the long spiritual trek of becoming godlike.

GOD'S HOLY LOVE

Although love is the most basic of God's attributes, His love does not violate His holiness. MacDonald takes a stern view of sin and insists that God doesn't overlook evil or minimize its consequences. All that displeases God in His children must be purged—not simply punished, for punishment's sake—and God's love effects the purging. In a sermon based upon Hebrews 12:29, "Our God is a consuming fire," he explains:

> Nothing is inexorable but love. Love which will yield to prayer is imperfect and poor. Nor is it then the love that yields, but its alloy. . . . For love loves unto purity. Love has ever in view the absolute loveliness of that which it beholds. Where loveliness is incomplete, and love cannot love its fill of loving, it spends itself to make more lovely, that it may love more; it strives for perfection, even that itself may be perfected—not in itself but in the object. . . .
>
> Therefore, all that is not beautiful in the beloved, all that comes between and is not of love's kind, must be destroyed.
>
> And our God is a consuming fire.[2]

This fire, then, is the very nature of God. It is remedial in nature, ever seeking to refine man, so that he will become more godlike. God's true children desire the work of this burning within them, relieving them of what is antagonistic to God in their inner beings. They therefore go toward God, cooperating with the process as best they know how. The rebellious will experience this fire in

2. "Our God is a Consuming Fire," *USI*, 27-28.

the next world more directly than they do in this one. The consuming fire of God eventually will consume all evil. But, as the chief spiritual mentor in *Lilith* explains, "Annihilation itself is no death to evil. Only good where evil was is evil dead. An evil thing must live with its evil until it chooses to be good. That alone is the slaying of evil." Evil men must come to choose good freely, not by coercion, and all evil within them must be replaced, by the process of growth, with good.

God's wrath, then, is hardly distinguishable from His love: both are creative. The anger of God is not on the side of those Scot Calvinists whose idea of holiness is sterile and pharisaical, and who feel somehow they have an exclusive claim upon God's love and mercy. God is against evil wherever it exists, evil which encrusts itself upon seemingly righteous people in subtle ways. But it is consumable, and must be consumed, that the essential nature of man, the image of God, may appear. When people are fully purged, they will be children of God in truth.

These ideas are thoroughly presented in MacDonald's sermons, and they are embodied throughout his imaginative writings. The symbolism in the two fantasies for children, *The Princess and the Goblin* and *The Princess and Curdie*, does not detail the entire process of spiritual growth, but it shadows forth many of these ideas. The great-great-grandmother, Queen Irene, and the manner of her working in the lives of spiritually sensitive individuals, the many types of creatures that arrange themselves on a scale of becoming, the strange fire of roses and its gift of "sensitive hands" bestowed upon Curdie—all these are pertinent to MacDonald's doctrine of becoming. In the manner of true art, these symbols do more than describe or illustrate these ideas: they present themselves imaginatively in a way that makes us feel their plausibility and power.

THE PRINCESS AND THE GOBLIN (1872)

Students of MacDonald tend to be fascinated with the extent to which his symbolic handling of the human psyche seems to anticipate Freud.[3] The hierarchy of the ancient grandmother, the princess, and the goblins does seem to suggest the superego, ego, and id, except that the goblins are not especially pleasure-loving, let alone libidinous. MacDonald in his writings often uses the metaphor of a castle for the human mind symbolizing the many rooms or facets of the psyche. His thinking is primarily Pauline.

The theme of this fantasy is that one must have a certain inner quality—a keen sensibility and childlike naiveté—in order to discern the spiritual nature of the universe and to maintain a trusting, joy-giving contact with higher spiritual powers that work for the good of man. We will see in a later chapter how Anodos, the hero of *Phantastes*, upon entering Faerie, could see the fairies in the wood only because he had the fairy nature. So in this story, an inner sensitivity is requisite to spiritual health and growth.

3. Reis, for instance, writes, "The Freudian hierarchy of ego (the Princess), superego (the Fairy Grandmother in the attic), and id (the Goblins in the basement) is obvious enough; and their presence reflects MacDonald's independent discovery of these phenomena" (81). See 41–45 for his discussion of the way in which MacDonald is one of those poets who "discovered" the subconscious prior to Freud.

The story presents a range of being, and hence of sensitivity, according to spiritual states, from the goblins—our baser selves—on the one hand to the old queen grandmother—our highest—on the other. The goblins are boorish, coarse-minded, and bungling, defeated by their own schemes, whereas the grandmother is altogether lovely and attractive. One of the most noteworthy aspects of MacDonald's talent is his ability to make good characters attractive, and this old lady is a good example.[4] Between these two extremes lie the other characters, and we like them to the degree that they are most like the grandmother queen, and least like the goblins.

In the symbolism of the fantasy, Queen Irene is a surrogate for the highest expression of being within man: God. She is Irene's grandmother—many times removed —and also named Irene, because the highest human, the quintessential Irene, is divine, being made in God's image. The grandmother lives a mysterious life apart in the highest recesses of the house, but the mystery of her activities becomes a source of utter delight to those who come to know about them. Her pervading reality subsumes all aspects of the lives of those who love and obey her, as she constantly works for their good, their spiritual betterment. The realization of this good, however, depends upon faith and obedience. Many have not the inner spiritual eyes that can see her, and sometimes even those who do have eyes seek and do not find her, a momentary failure that may be due to some disobedience

---

4. Speaking of the novels, Lewis writes: "One rare, and all but unique, merit . . . must be allowed. The 'good' characters are always the best and most convincing. His saints live. . . ." (*Anthology*, 18).

or neglect of one's present duty. MacDonald's emphasis is ever upon the necessity for active obedience that springs from childlike trust.

One must note, however, that these meetings with the old queen come at her bidding, not the princess's, and they are not simply the product of the princess's fancy. Rather, they occur to a person in "real life" when they are necessary to give strength and instruction for a certain task. The king, though of sufficient sensibility, is not required, as the princess is, to have an active role in the task depicted in this tale, and thus, although he is on good terms with the queen, she does not appear to him like she does to the princess. He explains to Irene: "'She has not invited me, you know, and great old ladies like her do not choose to be visited without leave asked and given.'"

People like Lootie, on the other hand, live by a skepticism that precludes their receiving such visits; she remains in spiritual dullness. She is, therefore, a threat to the princess's relation to the queen and hence must be told nothing about the experiences the princess is having with her. The danger she poses is that of dismissing the reality of the encounters, calling them mere dreams, and influencing the princess not to take them seriously. MacDonald persistently sees this skeptical rationalism that precipitates doubt as the greatest threat to healthy spirituality. The shadow image in *Phantastes* is an excellent example of this.

The opposite of this skepticism is the simply child-like spirit. When the princess asks her grandmother about the moon that is always shining upon her, she tells the wondering girl that "'if the light were to go out, you would fancy yourself lying in a bare garret, on a heap of old straw, and would not see one of the pleasant things around about you all the time.'" The moon seems to suggest the light of the pure, childlike imagination, without which the princess could not see the queen. The imagination is not unlike faith in MacDonald's thought; they seem to work together to achieve spiritual insight.

But even people who are on their way to becoming mature in goodness cannot see the old queen until they arrive at a certain state of sensitivity and openness to the supernatural. The experience of Curdie illustrates the point well. Perhaps the most fascinating scene in *The Princess and the Goblin* is that in which the princess with great expectation and enthusiasm takes Curdie to see the queen grandmother, only to discover to her chagrin that Curdie can see only a bare garret, a heap of musty straw, a sunbeam, and a withered apple. But Curdie is a boy made of the right stuff, and his encounter with the queen in the close of the story suggests he will have more such visits. The ending furnishes a handy base upon which MacDonald can build a sequel, which he does some ten years afterward in *The Princess and Curdie.*

THE PRINCESS AND CURDIE (1883)

The Princess and Curdie opens after a year has passed since the close of *The Princess and the Goblin.* The king and his princess have moved away to the capital, Gwyntystorm, and Curdie is sinking into spiritual mediocrity. He believes less and less in the "things he had never seen," thinking they belong to dreams and not to

the real world. Returning one evening from the mines
with his bow and arrow, he shoots a beautiful snow-white
pigeon. Immediately his conscience is troubled. Then, a
bright light shines around him from a silvery moon,
beckoning him to climb the tower in the castle and
come into the presence of Queen Irene. He obeys, the
wounded pigeon in his hand. She helps him to see himself as having lapsed into a state of being on the side of
wrong simply because he was "never wanting or trying to
be better," but always pleasing himself. She then points
him, through a series of interviews, to the path of true
spiritual development.

Chapters 3 through 8, in which Curdie's interviews
are presented, give graphic imaginative expression to
MacDonald's view of the nature of repentance, conversion, and faith. Curdie comes to see himself as taking the
wrong direction in life, turns toward goodness by a free
act of his will, and places himself at the old queen's
disposal, ready to obey her commands. She tests his
intentions by making a simple request: he must never
take sides with those who ridicule her. And when in any
trouble, he must come to her. "'I will see what I can do
for you,'" she promises, "'only the *canning* depends on
yourself.'" MacDonald is underscoring an essential point:
what divine power can accomplish for an individual depends
very much upon the attitude with which it is received.

Curdie's resolve is soon tested. The miners with
whom he works begin telling tales of "Old Mother
Wotherwop," attributing to her evil intentions and feats;
they are clearly referring to Queen Irene, crassly miscon-
ceiving her. Curdie remains quiet, and is soon prodded

and jeered for not agreeing. That evening, he lingers behind in the mine with his father when the rest of the miners retire. In the distance of the dark mine shaft, they see a pale green light, and, going toward it, they find themselves standing before the queen herself, appearing in the midst of an effulgent glory. To Curdie, "all he knew of the whole creation, seemed gathered in one centre of harmony and loveliness in the person of the ancient lady who stood before him in the very summer of beauty and strength." They are afforded this awesome and joyous vision because of the father's past faithfulness to truth and goodness, and because the queen has work for Curdie to do.

When Curdie remarks about the difference between her former appearance to him as an aged grandmother and her present beauty and strength, she tells Curdie that different people see her differently, according to their moral state: "'. . . it is one thing what you or your father may think about me, and quite another what a foolish or bad man may see in me.'" She continues to explain that if a thief were to see her as she is talking to Curdie, he would think he saw a demon: "'I should be all the same, but his evil eyes would see me as I was not.'" MacDonald seems to be imaginatively projecting a biblical principle, found, for instance, in Psalm 18, in which the Psalmist says of God: "With the loyal thou dost show thyself loyal . . . and with the crooked thou dost show thyself perverse." That Curdie and his father see her as glorious reflects their spiritual state; that the miners had referred to her as Old Mother Wotherwop, a witch, reflects theirs.

Nevertheless, the queen tells Curdie that the next time he sees her he may not at first recognize the shape in which she will appear. He pleads for a sign by which he may know her, and she refuses his request: "'. . . That would be to keep you from knowing me,'" she explains. "'It would be but to know the sign of me—not to know me myself . . . No; you must do what you can to know me, and if you do, you will.'" The fixed rigidity of a given sign or image must not be substituted for real meetings with the living Presence. The interview ends with the queen's bidding Curdie to come to her in her tower the following evening.

Attempts to go to the queen, however, are often foiled by barriers and difficulties. It was so for the princess in *The Princess and the Goblin,* and it is so for Curdie. As he makes his way to the tower the following night, he is detained outwardly by a stern doorkeeper, and inwardly by doubt. The figure of the self-appointed doorkeeper who would obstruct arbitrarily the path of the earnest soul is not an infrequent one in MacDonald's stories; apparently he means to condemn all clerics and ecclesiastical personnel who by various exclusive practices would interfere with, rather than help, those who seek God.

Curdie's doubt offers a larger threat to his coming into the presence of the queen. As he knocks on her door and is bid to enter, he opens the door to see only open sky and darkness, but no floor or walls. He stands dismayed, but decides to obey the queen's summons anyway, and as he steps forward, "that which had need of the floor found it, and his foot was satisfied." The scene may be viewed as vividly portraying the nature of faith, which is, as Curdie's example shows, simple active obedience to an explicit command, although the means to sustain that obedience may seem nowhere present to the human eye.

Within her presence, Curdie sees a vision of the old queen busy at a great spinning wheel, singing as she spins, and the ultimate source of the song is Curdie's own heart. The song foreshadows a future joy and loveliness greater than human language can express. It anticipates the Resurrection—"the time when the sleepers shall rise"—and celebrates a universal restoration of all things. As the song ends, the queen laughs, and her laugh is "sweeter than joy itself, for the heart of the laugh was love." That this song originates in Curdie's own heart reminds us that MacDonald's view of human nature was somewhat different from that of his Calvinist contemporaries, who believed in total depravity.

Two images in the room attract Curdie's immediate attention: the Silver Moon hanging above, and the great fire of burning roses on the hearth. We have already remarked about the moon. The fire of "glowing, flaming roses, red and white" is the same fire by which the princess Irene was partially cleansed in *The Princess and the Goblin*. Then only her clothes were cleansed, and not her hands and face, her immediate task not requiring the deeper preparation. But Curdie must be prepared for a larger and more demanding task, and his preparation is painful and terrifying. He is now commanded to thrust his hands directly into the fire; the resulting pain is indeed as much as he can bear. Were he to have pulled away, we are told, he would have been killed; spiritual trials are startlingly crucial, and unless they are met with steadfastness, they take their toll.

When the pain eventually subsides, he withdraws his hands to find they have become white and smooth and tender. The queen tells him he has received a supernatural gift, whereby he is now able by a handclasp to recognize the true spiritual state of a person who is becoming a beast; such a person he is not to trust. Conversely, if he feels a person's hand as "child-like," he knows he may trust him, for, however physically repulsive the person may appear, Curdie will know that he is becoming better within. This prophetic gift will enable him to fulfill his mission.

These images, which wield considerable mythic power, directly reflect many of MacDonald's convictions. The fire of roses suggests that those destined by God to perform a particular task must first be spiritually prepared. They are the truly "elect," a term MacDonald uses to designate those who are selected to service, rather than designating in a Calvinist sense those selected for salvation from hell. This service requires preparation: "A man can do nothing he is not fit to do," MacDonald writes in *Lilith*. The preparation consists first of purging and then of the bestowal of any strength or special gift required for the execution of the task. God makes His servants fit for His work by purging them of what in their lives may displease Him. They must be holy because he is holy; there is no other way. But God enlists people to perform His tasks because in love He allows them to have active part in creating the good that fulfills His purposes, and He provides the wherewithal for any task He requires. The burning in the fire of roses is one of MacDonald's more memorable symbolic scenes.

The controlling idea in this scene stands at the center of MacDonald's doctrine of becoming. He sees no magic whereby people are changed suddenly and easily for the better. To approach the burnings of divine holiness and be purged for true service is a costly experience to which only a few are selected.

But one does not bear the pain alone. The experience over, Curdie sees the queen has been weeping, and discovers she had suffered with him while his hands were being readied for service. We are reminded of Isaiah 63:8: "In all their affliction he was afflicted. . . ." God suffered with his people when they were suffering.[5] The Christian can suffer because Christ suffered, because God the Father suffers and will continue to suffer until all evil is annihilated. "Much good will come" from it all, as the queen lovingly tells Curdie.

The whole process, however, is not without risk. Curdie could have withdrawn his hands from the fire, to his own undoing. And as he goes to fulfill his mission he is not immune from spiritual peril, for the queen warns him: " '. . . if any one gifted with this perception once uses it for his own ends, it is taken from him, and then, not knowing that it is gone, he is in a far worse condition than before, for he trusts to what he has not got.' " The

5. MacDonald's thought emphasizes that Calvary *reveals* the sufferings of God on behalf of men: "What Jesus did, was what the Father is always doing; the suffering he endured was that of the Father from the foundation of the world, reaching its climax in the person of his Son. God provides the sacrifice; the sacrifice is himself. He is always, and has ever been sacrificing himself to and for his creatures. It lies in the very essence of his creation of them. The worst heresy, next to that of dividing religion and righteousness, is to divide the Father from the Son—in thought or feeling or action or intent; to represent the Son as doing that which the Father does not himself do" ("Life," *US II*). He is very careful to repudiate any theology that posits a tension between a wrathful Father and a merciful Son whose sufferings pacify the former.

threat of selfish motives negating true service is a constant one, as the queen again suggests in her final admonition to Curdie: "'I have one idea of you and your work, and you have another. . . . You must be ready to let my idea, which sets you working, set your idea right.'" Clearly, deference to the divine will is requisite to success.

Thus prepared, Curdie leaves on his mission. His task is to free the king and his daughter, and hence the kingdom, from destruction. His journey takes him to Gwyntystorm, the capital, and he finds the city to be in a state of spiritual degeneration, with the king and his daughter, the princess Irene, being held captive by usurpers. This may be MacDonald's best long fantasy for children.

Curdie completes his task in a city controlled by wicked men hostile to him and his purposes. When they are defeated, and the king is restored to his power, the king sentences them to be taken to the animals' country, with the pronouncement: "'Now shall ye be ruled with a rod of iron, that ye may learn what freedom is, and love it and seek it.'" Not fit for this world, they are sent into a lower one until they learn some basic moral truths. Gwyntystorm, liberated from evil, enjoys a reign of righteousness under the new king and queen, Irene and Curdie.

The generation following Irene and Curdie's, however, reverts to greed and self-centeredness, and Gwyntystorm is completely destroyed: only a river and a "wilderness of wild deer" remain where the city once stood. The continual potential of the human will to turn

away from God is real. In this story, the evil enticement
is a lust for gold, which shows the perceptive reader that
man cannot serve both God and mammon.[6]

6. Matthew 6:24. Woolf, convinced that MacDonald became disillusioned
with his own understanding of life as he grew older, sees this ending as evidence that MacDonald is "in an apocalyptic mood, striking out at what he
hates, and convinced that evil triumphs in the end" (*GK*, 176). But is not
MacDonald simply reminding his young readers that the conflict between
good and evil is continual, and thus those who do not keep growing spiritually, retrogress?

Chapter 3

Outward Signs Of Inward Grace

"'My boy! I doubt if you can tell what it is to know
the presence of the living God in and about you.'"
—Mr. Graham in *The Marquis of Lossie*

THE PRINCESS AND CURDIE opens with an impressive
passage of praise to mountains. They are "beautiful ter-
rors," having emerged from the dark heart of the earth to
stand majestic in the light of the sun. Inside, they are
filled with rich deposits of ores and precious stones
silently waiting to be discovered by man. As miners,
Curdie and his father live and work to bring to light
these "hidden things" and in so doing they are nourished
and sustained. Their lives are reliant upon nature. This
depiction typifies many of MacDonald's convictions
about the nature of earth and man's relation to it.

The term "sacramental" may be used in a very broad
sense, to describe MacDonald's view of God's relation to

both the world of nature and the world of event and circumstance. MacDonald himself uses this term in a passage from his early novel *The Portent*, and in so doing gives us the essence of his idea. He writes: "The very outside of a book had a charm to me. It was a kind of sacrament—an outward sign of an inward and spiritual grace; as, indeed, what on God's earth is not?"

A sacrament is an object or act that becomes a means whereby divine grace is, or may be, bestowed upon the recipient. Traditionally, Protestants reserve the term to refer to baptism and the Lord's Supper; Roman Catholics use it to describe seven essential rites of the Church. Whereas orthodox Christianity has tended to confine the application of the idea to very specific "sacred" acts, MacDonald suggests that it should have the widest possible application. Everything "on God's earth" is "an outward and visible sign of an inward and spiritual grace," in the sense that all circumstances and objects that surround people on any given day of their lives are invested by God with the potential to speak to them. Whether or not the potential that resides in a specific thing is realized by a person depends upon that individual's present stage of spiritual development, his sensibility, and his attitudes. But God in grace is continually shaping outward circumstances to one's inner needs. "That which is within a man, not that which lies beyond his vision, is the main factor in what is about to befall him: the operation upon him is the event," MacDonald observes in *Lilith*.

In fact, all that is within a person relates to all that is outside of him. MacDonald writes in *Orts*, a collection of his essays: "For the world is—allow us the homely figure—the human being turned inside out. All that moves in the mind is symbolized in Nature." These correspondences facilitate sacramental communication. A mystical life, a spirit from God Himself, courses through all nature and strives to communicate with man by using natural objects as symbols. In the novel *Thomas Wingfold* MacDonald states:

> All about us, in earth and air, wherever the eye or ear can reach, there is a power ever breathing itself forth in signs, now in wind-waft, a cloud, a sunset; a power that holds constant and sweetest relation with the dark and silent world within us. The same God who is in us, and upon whose tree we are the buds, if not yet the flowers, also is all about us—inside the Spirit; outside, the Word. And the two are ever trying to meet in us. . . .

By virtue of the immanence of God in all things, as well as within man, there is a unity of substance between each man and the symbols he sees.[1]

1. *Thomas Wingfold*, Chapter 82. Reis sees antecedents for "MacDonald's views of God's self-expression in nature" in Emanuel Swedenborg, Jakob Böhme, and William Law (38) William Blake could have been listed as well. Like so much nineteenth-century thought that speculates on the relation of the physical to the spiritual, MacDonald's conception derives in part from Swedenborg's thinking, such as is found in his *Heaven and Hell*. Greville writes that his father "knew enough of Swedenborg's teaching to feel the truth of *correspondences*, and would find innumerable instances of physical law tallying with metaphysical, of chemical affinities with spiritual affections . . ." (*GMDW*, 216; italics his). Thus Swedenborg seems to be the fountainhead of some of MacDonald's ideas, with some influence provided by Blake and Law. But his thought is most directly shaped by the German Romantics. Inasmuch as the French Symbolists also drew somewhat upon the thought of Swedenborg and the Germans, parallels may be drawn between the French Symbolists' idea of correspondences and MacDonald's. Yet in the material

MacDonald's theory of the nature of literary symbols is a direct extension of this thinking. As the poet uses images from nature, he reveals the thoughts of God resident in nature, and his work captures "truth in beauty"—MacDonald's definition for poetry.[2] The more a poet grows into spiritual maturity, the more his thoughts reflect God's truths, and hence the more potent his symbols become as sacraments. They are the vehicles of the truths God has given him to perceive and communicate. Further, in MacDonald's view neither the thoughts nor the images conveying them may be said to be original with man. They arise from the "unconscious portion of his nature," and "God sits in that chamber" of man's being. Man in his subconscious being, therefore, does not exist independently from God. God made man out of Himself, MacDonald felt, and man lives and moves and has his being in God.[3]

available to me, there is no evidence of MacDonald's drawing directly upon the French. The distinctive character of MacDonald's thought, and its chief interest for this study, is the evangelical-pietistic emphasis MacDonald gives to this current of idea. Greville explains: "Once, forty years ago, I held conversation with my father on the laws of symbolism. He would allow that the algebraic symbol, which concerns only the three-dimensional, has no *substantial* relation to the unknown quantity; nor the 'tree where it falleth' to the man unredeemed, the comparison being false. But the rose, when it gives some glimmer of the freedom for which a man hungers, does so because of its *substantial* unity with the man, each in degree being a signature of God's immanence" (*GMDW*, 482; italics his).

2. *ADO*, 15.

3. *ADO*, 24, 25. "I repent me of the ignorance wherein I ever said that God made man out of nothing: there is no nothing out of which to make anything; God is all in all, and he made us out of himself. He who is parted from God has no original nothingness with which to take refuge. He is a live discord, an anti-truth. He is a death fighting against life . . ." (*Weighed and Wanting*, Chapter 35). Thus MacDonald repudiates the doctrine of creation ex nihilo, which Augustine taught, and which many orthodox theologians have believed. Cf. Acts 17:28.

One may observe that there is a large potential in MacDonald's thought for his claiming personal distinction and thus using his works to pontificate: "Stand thou there and be attentive while my works bless you." But he is never guilty of this. Next to the theme of the necessity for constant obedience to known duty, perhaps no theme is stronger in his works than that of the necessity of humility. He felt God allowed even the best of men but fleeting glimpses of truth in this life, and that men in future ages will see truths still more clearly. The deepest things of God are "far too simple for us to understand as yet.⁴ For these reasons he was content to let his works speak for themselves—but he does insist that spiritual health for any man depends upon his maintaining the closest possible bond between himself and the natural world.

Many scenes in the novels and adult fantasies clearly depict these ideas about the sacramental relation of all things to man. Examples of episodes showing man interacting with nature occur in *Sir Gibbie* (Gibbie in the thunderstorm), *Robert Falconer* (Robert Falconer in the Alps), and *Phantastes* ("All that man sees has to do with man", chapter 12). Just after the hero Anodos leaves the Cottage of the Four Oaks and is walking through the woods, all the plants seem inhabited by fleeting presences that are watching him. He observes:

> From the lilies, . . . from the campanulas, from the foxgloves, and every bell-shaped flower, curious little figures shot up their heads, peeped at me, and drew back. They seemed to inhabit them . . . and I heard

4. *ADO*, 18.

them saying to each other, evidently intending me to hear, but the speaker always hiding behind his tuft, when I looked in his direction, "Look at him! Look at him! He has begun a story without a beginning, and it will never have any end. . . ."

All nature is interested in the being and destiny of Anodos. In chapter 24, after Anodos is slain in his noble attempt to battle the vicious powers of a religious ritualism, he is buried by his friends the knight and the marble lady "amid many trees," during the growth and verdure of springtime. In a monologue, Anodos tells us:

> Now that I lay in her bosom, the whole earth, and each of her many births, was as a body to me, at my will. I seemed to feel the great heart of the mother beating into mine, and feeding me with her own life, her own essential being and nature. . . . I rose into a single large primrose that grew by the edge of the grave, and from the window of its humble, trusting face, looked full in the countenance of the lady. I felt that I could manifest myself in the primrose; that it said a part of what I wanted to say; just as in the old time, I had used to betake myself to a song for the same end. The flower caught her eye. She stooped and plucked it, saying, "Oh, you beautiful creature!"

Anodos assumes other natural forms as well—in one instance becoming a cloud—for the purpose of ministering to men. He exults that he now can "love without needing to be loved again," and he then expresses his newly achieved insights into the power and beauty of love.

Anodos, being "dead," is able to realize experientially this power of love beyond any realization he had during his earthly life. The scene underscores the strength and extent of MacDonald's sacramentalism. Human attempts to love effectively may be hampered and rendered imperfect by the limitations inherent in the human condition; inanimate things may love with more abandon. In a scene near the beginning of Anodos's wanderings, in which he is enveloped by the arms of a beech tree, the tree croons: "'I may love him, I may love him; for he is a man, and I am only a beech-tree.'" Removed from any suggestions of sensuality or self-advantage, the tree is able as a natural object to serve Anodos's present need to be loved more completely.

In the final chapter of *Phantastes*, Anodos is once again in his "bodily and earthly life," and the book closes with his seeking a momentary respite from his labor in the fields under an ancient beech tree. Reclining there and listening to the sound of the leaves in the breeze, he seems to hear them say: "'A great good is coming—is coming—is coming to thee, Anodos.'" The fantasy then closes with this confidence: "Yet I know that good is coming to me—that good is always coming; though few have at all times the simplicity and the courage to believe it. What we call evil, is the only and best shape, which, for the person and his condition at the time, could be assumed by the best good." Even evil, in its effects, may be a word of God to a man. All MacDonald's writings may be said to have as their end the creating within his readers of "the simplicity and courage to believe it."

AT THE BACK OF THE NORTH WIND (1871)

That evil, in the form of adverse circumstances and events, may be sacramental is a strong theme in the children's fantasy *At the Back of the North Wind.* The conclusion from *Phantastes* would also serve as an excellent statement of the controlling idea for this novel-length fantasy. The imagery of the title suggests the equivocal nature of adversity, the north wind being a common image for what is adverse and unpleasant. However, to be at its back—that is, going with it rather than against it— is, as the story soon makes clear, a fascinating and salutary place to be.

Diamond is the small son of a poor London coach-man, and his bedroom is a rickety structure built over the coach-house affording meager protection from the cutting blasts of the North Wind. One particular night when the rushing wind is whistling shrilly around Diamond's bed, he seems to hear it speaking to him. Engaging it in conversation, he discovers the wind to be a fascinating woman of mighty beauty, with both anger and sweetness mingled in her looks. From her face comes light, as from the moon. On succeeding nights he accompanies her, flying with her over London ensconced in her long hair, while she fulfills her assignments. She carries out the bidding of a Higher Power, whose ways she herself does not firmly understand.

When he is confident she is not cruel, but good-intentioned, he asks her how it is she can bear to bring disaster, such as her present task of sinking a ship. She answers that she hears above the noise of the immediate disaster the "sound of a far-off song" that quite satisfies her concerning the present suffering, for it tells her that "all is right." When Diamond objects that what comforts her doesn't do her victims much good, she counters: " 'It must. It must. It wouldn't be the song it seems to be if it did not swallow up all their fear and pain too, and set them singing it themselves with the rest.' " The theme that good can come of ill, illustrated in the opening scene, is woven throughout the course of Diamond's ensuing experiences.

Before the story reverts to realism, Diamond is taken to see the country at the back of the North Wind. The story makes clear that the trip occurs while he is seriously ill, and in a delirious state. She takes him far into the regions of the North, and then, in a memorable scene, he is commanded to pass directly through her person. Doing so, he enters a higher land in which nothing is wrong, but neither is anything quite right. This region, however, is pervaded with the certainty that everything is "going to be right some day." It is a land where there is peace and contentment intermingled with a patient waiting for a future fulfillment. The "good" dead are there, able to observe their loved ones back on earth, while anticipating fuller bliss in the Resurrection to come.

The experience of being in this higher land gives Diamond a moral and spiritual maturity beyond that normally acquired by anyone in this life, so that when he returns to health and the story progresses, he is shown to be a model of virtue. With impeccable obedience and industry Diamond works altruistically for the good of the poor, the sick, and the unfortunate—society's castoffs in the streets of nineteenth-century London. MacDonald's purpose is to show him realizing a fully harmonious cooperation with the principle that adversity and disaster are controlled by a power that uses them as channels and instruments for ultimate good. It is an intriguing purpose, but it is difficult, if not impossible, to work out in a believable manner in this more realistic section. For this reason, this portion of the novel is considerably less appealing than the former section of the fantasy.

It would seem, then, that symbolic art can succeed in fulfilling such a purpose where realistic art cannot. The wanderings of Anodos in *Phantastes*, although they seem to be aimless, haphazard, and sometimes terrifying, all work for his ultimate good, while at the same time the reader delights in the imaginative fantasy world of Faerie. Similarly, as long as *At the Back of the North Wind* maintains a semifantastic setting, it also is charming and convincing; but at the point at which it seeks to demonstrate its theme in the real world of London coachmen, it fails to satisfy one's sense of reality.

This artistic dilemma is underscored by the success of the fairy tale "Little Daylight," which MacDonald inserts into the plot of the book. A kindly poet who befriends Diamond visits a children's hospital and tells the patients there a fairy tale, the theme of which reinforces that of the book. "'I never knew of any interference on the part of the wicked fairy that did not turn out a good thing in the end,'" the narrator announces, and proceeds to tell the story of a princess named Little Daylight. At her christening, a wicked fairy cursed her, dooming her to sleep all day and to wake only at night, and then to be strong or weak according to the waxing or waning of the moon. Thus she grows up into a beautiful

princess, dancing in the moonlight forests but never
seeing the sun. A noble prince, who sees her in her nocturnal dances, falls in love with her. Later discovering her
on a moonless night weak and ugly because of the curse,
he befriends her, completely unaware that she is the same
beautiful princess he has seen dancing, and out of pity he
kisses her. The spell is thus broken, and her beauty
returns, together with the privilege of at last enjoying the
sun and, it is intimated, the prince's love. This tale is
pleasant and satisfying, temporarily suspending any
reluctance the reader may feel toward accepting the
larger thesis of the book.

The book recovers its charm in the closing chapters.
Diamond's illness returns, and he dies. North Wind
resumes her nocturnal visits to Diamond during his
illness, and his death is depicted as his making a final
trip to the "back of the North Wind." The aura of her
presence in these closing scenes lingers in the mind, and
many of her speeches give memorable expression to some
of MacDonald's basic ideas. For instance, she answers
Diamond's inquiry about whether dreams are to be
trusted: "'The people who think lies, and do lies, are very
likely to dream lies. But the people who love what is true
will surely now and then dream true things. But then
something depends on whether the dreams are home-
grown, or whether the seed of them is blown over
somebody else's garden wall. . . .'" Good people should
trust their own deepest feelings and treasure their own
highest hopes. How they shall come to fruition is a
mystery, but one may safely hope they shall. Diamond
articulates this hope in a song about the seasons:

> Sure is the summer,
> Sure is the sun;
> The night and the winter
> Are shadows that run.

MacDonald's view of the sacramental character of nature and event combines with his belief in the essential goodness of man's primary feelings and passions to produce a view of human experience different from that of some traditions in historic Christianity. It opposes the ascetic tradition and solidly challenges the essentially Platonic assumptions upon which that tradition is based. MacDonald could not accept the view that there exists an irreconcilable enmity between body and spirit, and that the body must be severely checked and chastised for the good of the soul. For him, what people must pit their spiritual energies against is the inferior selves of their beings, the undersides of their natures. The enemy is within us, is indeed *ourselves*.

Chapter 4

Wells and Cisterns:
Phantastes

"I knew now, that it is by loving, and not by being loved,
that one can come nearest the soul of another. . . ."
—Anodos in *Phantastes*

C. S. Lewis TELLS OF HIS first discovery of
Phantastes and of the change it made in his life:

It must be more than thirty years ago that I bought—
almost unwillingly, for I had looked at the volume on
the book-stall and rejected it on a dozen previous
occasions—the Everyman edition of Phantastes. A
few hours later I knew that I had crossed a great fron-
tier. . . . What it actually did to me was to convert,
even to baptise . . . my imagination. . . . The quality
which had enchanted me in his imaginative works
turned out to be the quality of the real universe, the

77

divine, magical, terrifying and ecstatic reality in which
we all live.[1]

Lewis had crossed into the land of Faerie, the land of all
MacDonald's fantasies. It is a higher land, existing in the
imagination, and entered by a willingness to leave the
actual world behind and to follow the author on an
adventure in which anything can happen. Following the
example of Edmund Spenser in *The Faerie Queene,*
MacDonald presents Faerie as a land shaped by spiritual
principles, which enables him to view all human experience upon an anagogic level. But rather than presenting
an allegorical tale, as Spenser did, MacDonald shapes a
myth by means of deftly chosen symbols and an ethereal
tone.

In his letters to Arthur Greeves written before his
conversion to Christianity, C. S. Lewis often talks of the
effects which MacDonald's writing were having upon
him. "I know nothing that gives me such a feeling of
spiritual healing, of being washed, as to read G.
Macdonald," he confided. *Phantastes* was clearly his
favorite among MacDonald's works.[2] What was effecting
him was the dynamic of myth. MacDonald took his
inspiration for writing fairy tales from the German
Romantic writer Novalis and appended it to *Phantastes* as
an epigraph. It calls for a narrative surface, busy and
incoherent, supported by an underlying musical
harmony. The subsurface harmony derives from an
orchestration of themes. The result is a tale that works
upon the reader sacramentally.

1. *Anthology,* 20, 21.
2. *They Stand Together: The Letters of C. S. Lewis to Arthur Greeves (1914–1963),*
ed. Walter Hooper. (London: Collins, 1979) 389.

For a fantasy to function at its best sacramentally, MacDonald felt that a person should read it simply for his own pleasure, not consciously for his edification, as he would read, say, a parable. It is, of course, intuitive perceptions that MacDonald has in mind. Mere intellectual analysis alone tends to leave the spirit emaciated, not strengthened. Some incidents will seem to convey moral and spiritual truths—others will remain incorrigibly enigmatic. The type and quantity of truths perceived will depend upon the reader's spiritual state and special needs at the time.

To approach the text correctly readers must allow the tale to activate their imaginations. In tracing the themes one is able to observe the underlying harmony. In *Phantastes,* the main theme appears to address the problem of man's search for satisfactions for his personal desires and longings. The Christian concern arises because the natural process of seeking satisfactions for human desires is self-centered, and self-centeredness is spiritually destructive.

What is man to do? MacDonald does not advocate the classic answer of Christian asceticism—that human passions are to be repressed, and many natural satisfactions denied. He shows, rather, that it is better to serve others than ourselves, and that our desires can be satisfied indirectly through this service. Real love endeavors to give, not get, and in so doing, finds inner satisfactions that self-centered love cannot begin to know, together with a joy not otherwise attained. This theme is summarized in a poem found in chapter 19:

> Better to sit at the waters' birth,
> Than a sea of waves to win;
> To live in the love that floweth forth,
> Than the love that cometh in.
>
> Be thy heart a well of love, my child,
> Flowing, and free, and sure;
> For a cistern of love, though undefiled,
> Keeps not the spirit pure.

Spiritual maturity consists in being like a well that gives and is always fresh, rather than like a cistern that is full to stagnation. How one becomes the former and avoids being the latter is carefully illustrated in the hero's adventures.

THE HERO

The hero of *Phantastes*, Anodos, undergoes a series of adventures in Fairy Land, each of which helps him to grow morally and spiritually. His name itself is instructive, being a transliteration from a Greek word which has two meanings: "having no way" and "rising."[3] Anodos wanders through Faerie in a seemingly aimless manner, but all that happens to him has the power to make him rise, or grow, so that he is in the process of becoming a better person.

He enters Faerie when he turns twenty-one, and he remains in that land twenty-one days; in other words, having reached physical and legal maturity, he is brought by his adventures to moral and spiritual maturity as well. In order to grow, Anodos must accept the reality of Fairy

3. Liddell and Scott, *A Greek-English Lexicon*, rev. ed. (Oxford: Oxford University Press, 1940), 145.

Land, the supernatural world. This requires both a certain inherent sensibility and a desire to cultivate it. At the beginning of the adventures, Anodos is concerned whether he has "fairy blood" and whether he can see the fairies in the woods. He learns from the lips of the country maiden whom he meets in chapter 4 that he could not have come so far in the woods if he did not have "fairy blood" within him. She takes him into the Cottage of the Four Oaks to her mother, who tells him that his ability to appreciate Fairy Land and to see the fairies there is determined by the strength of his fairy nature. He is much concerned about himself until he discovers that he can in fact see the fairies clearly. His fascination with their antics and affairs in the remainder of the chapter shows us that Anodos is indeed the right type of person to profit from these adventures. His having fairy blood does not, in itself, indicate that he has attained moral maturity; rather, it reveals that he fits the type of one who may acquire it.

In chapter 1 Anodos's attitudes and concerns reveal his need for spiritual growth. He is a young man who desires material and physical things. The story opens with his awakening in bed, and his morning thoughts concern his "legal rights," because he is in the process of inheriting wealth from his deceased father. He recalls that the day before, as he was searching through his father's things, he was interrupted by a visit from a tiny "womanform," who generated within him certain desires, both admirable and unadmirable.

In his conversation with her, he makes three mistakes: he hesitates to believe in her because he has seen her only once; he belittles her because of her smallness; and, when she accommodates his prejudices and becomes "normal" size, he is physically attracted to her and tries to embrace her. These mistakes rest upon assumptions common to ordinary people in the world at large. The first is that the authority of any supernatural event is strengthened by the number of times it is repeated, an assumption to which the scientific mind is inclined. The second is that the larger something is, the more important it must be, an assumption made by many people. The third is that what is physically attractive must be immediately possessed, an assumption made by sensual people.

For these mistakes, he receives her rebukes. The rebuke to his sensuality is strengthened by her suggesting that she may be the spirit of one of his deceased grandmothers. The suggestion increases the mystery that surrounds her, and Anodos, looking into her eyes, is filled with an "unknown longing" for Fairy Land, which she assures him he will find tomorrow.

What is happening here must be carefully noted, for it suggests a pattern for much that follows. Two types of desire—the one for sexual gratification, and the other for joyous experiences in the supernatural world—follow rapidly one upon another, and both are associated with the same woman. MacDonald suggests that, for man in a low state of spiritual development, these two desires are not all that different from each other. Anodos must learn to distinguish carefully between them and handle each one correctly. This theme is worked out in detail in the episodes of Anodos's experiences with his marble lady, and is orchestrated in both the story of Cosmo in chapter 13 and "The Ballad of Sir Aglovaile" in chapter 19.

One should note as well, in this important opening chapter, the use of male and female figures as symbols. The fairy woman tells Anodos: " 'I dare say you know something of your great-grandfathers a good deal further back. . . ; but you know very little about your great-grandmothers on either side.' " Apparently, male ancestors symbolize the concerns of the everyday and commercial world; female ones symbolize the less known, mysterious side of experience. It is through delving into the mysteries of life that one reaches the higher truths—so elusive and difficult to express, yet so nourishing to the human spirit—that give meaning to existence. One recalls the presentation of the female figure in the Curdie books and in *At the Back of the North Wind:* in the former, the aged queen Irene is both the essential human and the divine; in the latter, the North Wind acts as Diamond's entrance into the higher realm of life beyond death. Frequently in the fantasies, women have finer natures and keener sensibilities than men, guarding truth and guiding men to it. Therefore, physical desires which men feel toward women, kept chaste and tastefully expressed, are ready symbols of man's deep longing to possess a knowledge of ultimate truth.[4]

MacDonald presents two attitudes toward sexual desire. In its baser form as lewd and promiscuous desire, he condemns it as being a certain evidence of need for moral and spiritual development. But in its higher expressions—regulated according to Christian principles—it is an aid to moral and spiritual development.

4. MacDonald's thinking on the role of women in spiritual experience bears interesting relation to that of Charles Williams. Cf. *The Figure of Beatrice* and his novels.

Elsewhere in his writings (see, for instance, the essay "Individual Development" in *Orts,* or the novel *Paul Faber, Surgeon*), he makes clear that a proper sensuality may become a means of renewing one's conviction of the reality of the spiritual world.

FIRST ADVENTURES

We believe with delight in Anodos's entrance into Faerie, feeling wonder with him as the items in his bedroom gradually change into the natural surroundings of the new land. As soon as he is within this land of the imagination, he meets a country maiden who warns him concerning the trees: " 'Trust the Oak, and the Elm, and the great Beech. Take care of the Birch, for though she is honest, she is too young not to be changeable. But shun the Ash and the Alder; for the Ash is an ogre—you will know him by his thick fingers; and the Alder will smother you with her web of hair, if you let her near you at night.' " The warning is dramatic, preparing us for fierce conflicts between good and evil beings, both interested in Anodos's allegiances. In Anodos's later meeting with the beech tree, we learn of "an old prophecy" that trees will one day become men and women. Clearly the life that animates all of nature is full of significance for man, both for the present and the future.

Four oak trees form the corners of the first cottage he sees, indicating the trustworthiness of the country maiden's mother who dwells there. She, too, warns him about the ash tree, but avoids being specific about the danger; all she will say is that the ash's favorite tactic is to kill his victims with fright. The reader is deep within the story before discovering the precise nature of the evil that the ash represents: the spiritual disaster which comes from being consumed with a selfish sensuality.

Another important person in Anodos's spiritual education is now introduced: the knight, Sir Percival. In the cottage Anodos discovers a large old book containing "many wondrous tales of Fairy Land," and in it he reads a fragment of the legend of Sir Percival. It pictures Sir Galahad, in shining armor, meeting Sir Percival, whose armor is red with rust and whose horse is "smirched with mud and mire." Percival's condition is a result of his seduction by the "damosel of the alder-tree." The account reinforces the warning given Anodos concerning the evil trees and suggests the danger he too will face.

Fleeing in horror from the spirit of the pursuing ash tree, Anodos stumbles and falls, stunned, at the root of a large beech. Suddenly he is enveloped by "two large soft arms" and hears the reassuring voice of a woman murmuring, " 'I may love him, I may love him; for he is a man, and I am only a beech tree.' " After giving him a tress of her hair to protect him from the dangers of the ash, she sings:

> I saw thee ne'er before;
> I see thee never more;
> But love, and help, and pain, beautiful one,
> Have made thee mine, till all my years are done.

Love that gives of itself—that helps another though that help means personal pain—unlocks the secret of life and bliss. This, Anodos comments, is the "secret of the

woods, and the flowers, and the birds." It is a far cry from
the love that desires to possess another for the satisfaction of selfish passions.

Spiritually exhilarated by this experience, Anodos
next discovers his marble lady. While walking through a
seemingly friendly portion of the wood, he enters a
mossy cave for rest. He begins to daydream, thinking
about "lovely forms, and colors, and sounds," until he
realizes he is lying on a moss-covered block of alabaster.
When he removes the moss from his couch, he is startled
to find that it encases the marble form of a sleeping
woman; she is perfectly lovely. Seized with a deep desire
to awaken the woman, he finds himself "rejoicing in a
song" and begins to sing. The power of his songs is effective; she arises and flees, with Anodos following. (The
power of song will be further discussed in the final
chapter of this study.)

The incident pictures Anodos possessed by desire or
love in its highest and purest form. The marble lady
appears to symbolize the spirit of the Ideal, or the
Perfect, that acts as an innate guide to God. She is the
spirit that weds perfect beauty and ultimate truth.
Something deep within Anodos's soul answers to her: he
comments that her perfect loveliness was "more near the
face that had been born with me in my soul, than anything I had seen before in nature or art." These deep
longings toward the Ideal are an important aspect of the
theory of Romantic art. At the time that he wrote
Phantastes, MacDonald was the fledgling artist, with
growing convictions about the power of literary art to
perceive and express spiritual truths. Anodos mirrors

him: he is a singer whose songs have on this occasion freed the marble lady, and will evoke her later. Anyone who entertains an ideal and expends his energies pursuing it will find that Anodos's experiences serve as a mirror, showing much about oneself.

FACING INITIAL DANGERS

The ideal is fleeting and elusive. One is compelled by love to follow it, but the way is beset with spiritual pitfalls. Each pitfall Anodos faces is a variation on the theme of the nature of love. When love's energies flow exclusively toward the self, they are spiritually disastrous; only when its energies flow outward, so that all self-centered considerations are obliterated, can one commune satisfyingly with his ideal. The end of such selfless devotion to the ideal is union with it. Anodos summarizes at the end of chapter 22 what he learns: ". . . my ideal soon became my life; whereas, formerly, my life had consisted in a vain attempt to behold, if not my ideal in myself, at least myself in my ideal."

The first of Anodos's vain attempts to selfishly possess the ideal results in his falling into the hands of the Maid of the Alder. After he again meets Sir Percival, who warns him to beware of her, he resolves to profit from the knight's example, but nevertheless goes straight to his undoing. He composes another song, and a white lady immediately appears. The substance of the song, however, is quite different from the theme of the former ones: it addresses the "Queen of the Night" and asks to be secluded with her in a night of love. On the story level, Anodos is showing the same animal sensuality that he

showed in the opening chapter toward his "grandmother" from Faerie. MacDonald has already warned
against such passion, and will continue to do so in many
episodes yet to come.

In this episode, the reader is subtly but definitely
made concerned for Anodos's safety. First, in his song he
dismisses the moon, hoping it will not rise this particular
night. A frequent and complex symbol in MacDonald's
writings, the moon here seems to suggest the beneficent
providence of God that pervades the universe. For
Anodos, it functions throughout his adventures as his
guardian spirit. For him to dismiss it indicates he is
laying himself open to danger. As he does so he feels a
certain uneasiness, but he ignores it, yielding to the
sensuous pull of the moment.

As the marble lady takes Anodos to her grotto, he is
enchanted with her "intense loveliness" and "extreme
beauty." His sensual longings show him to be in a spiritual state of complete self-centeredness. Lying entranced
with her loveliness, he is engrossed in the tale she tells
him, in which he and she are the principal characters. He
becomes ecstatic as he surrenders himself to self-centered
imaginings.

But Anodos awakes from his swoon in the gray dawn
to be confronted with horror. (In the dream world of
Faerie, beauty and ugliness, the ethereal and the
grotesque, can be swiftly juxtaposed without offending
the reader's credulity.) His marble lady has become the
Maid of the Alder. She appears now at the mouth of the
cave "like an open coffin set up on one end . . . a rough
representation of the human frame, only hollow," tearing

at hair held in her hands. She commits the terrified Anodos to her monstrously ghoulish companion, the Ash tree. The famed Maid of the Alder has undone the knight and now purposes to destroy him. About to be seized by the Ash, Anodos is narrowly saved when "the dull, heavy blow of an axe" echoes through the woods, and the tree shudders, groans, and then flees. The Maid of the Alder, with a disdainful look, flees as well. Exhausted and dejected, Anodos, too, leaves the cave, a perplexed and humbled man. How, he asks himself, can "beauty and ugliness dwell so near"?

Anodos remembers the warning given him upon entering Faerie: "'. . . the Alder will smother you with her web of hair, if you let her near you at night.'" So, too, the warning of the beech-tree maiden is fulfilled, who had admonished him there were beings in the wood whom he should beware of, and he should try to avoid the "very beautiful." His unpracticed eye was deceived into mistaking the Maid of the Alder for his marble lady. He unwisely pursued what was beautiful for selfish rather than selfless ends. His mistake has almost meant his death, for all selfishness is spiritually destructive.

THE CHALLENGE OF RATIONALISM AND DOUBT

Another pitfall for those pursuing their ideals is that of succumbing to a sterile, analytical rationality. It may offer a challenge to the existence of the entire supernatural world, as the episode in the farmer's cottage does, or it may be destructively analytical of one's experiences, robbing the reader of the joy he should otherwise know, as the many incidents of the shadow plaguing Anodos suggest. In any case, this cynicism is a result of self-centeredness.

In the next adventure, Anodos accepts the hospitality of a farm family. The mother is a devotee of Faerie lore, and the daughter is fascinated with fairy stories; the husband, however, believes all fairy matter to be a hoax, and the son agrees, adding contempt to his father's denials. Through these two characters MacDonald shows the antagonism of empiricism and rationalism to all imaginative activities. The temptation is to disbelieve in Fairy Land altogether, viewing it as only a delusion. The farmer is the congenial "outsider" who simply lacks the capacity to perceive anything intuitively. It is ironic, of course, that he himself dwells in the very land the existence of which he would deny.

Leaving the farmer's family in a despondent mood, Anodos goes deeper into the forest and comes upon a hut, built against a tall cypress (symbol of dejection), and enters. It is the house of the ogre, against whom the farmer has warned him. That the warning came from the male symbol of rationality suggests that no fine discrimination is required to avoid this danger. Within, Anodos finds a woman reading aloud from an ancient volume, a philosophy of negation and despair, the very opposite of all MacDonald himself teaches.

This dark philosophy, together with Anodos's mood, causes his cynical self to emerge. Probing in the cottage, Anodos comes upon a closet door which opens to "a narrow, dark passage." As he peers into the darkness, a "dark figure" runs toward him and, to Anodos's alarm, fastens itself to him as his shadow. The woman tells him that anyone who has come from a meeting such as his recent one in the forest is almost certain to be visited by his shadow. That is, Anodos there encountered his ideal— his marble lady—and he is now beset by its opposite, his lower self. Until Anodos masters the shadow with a spirit of humility at the end of chapter 22 (" 'I have lost myself—would it had been my shadow.' I looked round: the shadow was nowhere to be seen"), it intervenes and interferes in various incidents, defeating the good that could otherwise issue, and often working definite harm.

The possibility of possessing many selves is a basic theme in MacDonald's thought, and will be developed further in *Lilith*. The "self" in this sense is not man's true person, but rather its negative underside, and control by the self is an open possibility for an individual, not a necessity. This idea is directly related to MacDonald's doctrine of becoming: each of the successive possibilities of inferior selfhood must be met and successfully denied as one journeys spiritually toward oneness with God. That Anodos's shadow emerges when it does is itself a mark of Anodos's spiritual growth, an indicator that he has so far advanced in inner development that his true self is beginning to be aware of a lower self that, when indulged, negates good and works harm. That the shadow most often expresses a cynical "common sense" or worldly-wise attitude underscores MacDonald's insistence that a healthy Christian spirit is a childlike, imaginative one. [5]

5. After a presentation of the doppelgänger tradition upon which MacDonald seems to be drawing, Woolf laments that MacDonald shifts the symbolic significance of the shadow from "intellectual skepticism" to "consciousness of self" to personal "pride" (*GK*, 103). Reis agrees, concluding that the shadow's "symbolic meanings are multifold," but acknowledges a "subtle unity among

As he continues his journey Anodos finds that now his relation to all things is affected by his shadow. When he rests on the grass, the flowers upon which he lies revive; those the shadow lies upon do not. His attendant appears "blacker in the full blaze of sunlight," and, as Anodos's fascination for his shadow increases, it becomes so bold as to smite "the great sun in the face." The sun seems to be a symbol for God, the source of all spiritual light; the shadow is doubt, rooted in rational analysis.

Succeeding incidents in chapter 9 reveal the shadow's disastrous effects: he transforms the mysterious into the commonplace, and creates distrust between friends. Soon Anodos begins to think the shadow is indispensable to his well-being. He says to himself:

> In a land like this, with so many illusions everywhere, I need his aid to disenchant the things around me. He does away with all appearances, and shows me things in their true color and form. And I am not one to be fooled with the vanities of the common crowd. I will not see beauty where there is none. I will dare to behold things as they are. And if I live in a waste instead of a paradise, I will live knowing where I live.

This is the creed of the cynic, a result of a "common sense" approach to life. It is an avowed enemy of the visions of the imagination.

This conclusion leads Anodos to injure another by being crassly inconsiderate. In the forest he meets a little

the significances" (93). He also sees similarities to Jung's "Shadow" archetype (116, 117). The point is, it seems to me, that these various manifestations of the shadow's nature are all consistent aspects of the cynical underside of Anodos's character with which he will contend throughout much of the tale, and which he outgrows spiritually through humility and altruism. Consult the sermons "Self-Denial" (*US II*) and "The Heirs of Heaven and Earth" (*HG*).

maiden, happy and dancing, who carries a small crystal globe. Touching the globe makes it pour forth a torrent of harmonious music. (It probably symbolizes the imagined story-world of a child's delight.) The girl is most gentle with the globe, but Anodos, emboldened by his shadow, seizes it, and it bursts. The child is heart-broken, and Anodos is thereafter haunted by the incident, until he meets her again later in his adventures.

Another result—but Anodos says he is not certain this one is owing to the shadow—is that people become grotesque to him when he gets very close to them: "I soon found that . . . to feel I was in pleasant company, it was absolutely necessary for me to discover and observe the right focal distance between myself and each one with whom I had to do." The suggestion is that analyzing people too closely mars human relationships. To love others requires seeing them imaginatively, not only as they are but as they are capable of becoming.

THE FAIRY PALACE

Just as a stream flowing through Anodos's bedroom took him into Fairy Land, so now he discovers a streamlet which, as he follows it, leads him to the Marble Palace at the center of Faerie. Before he arrives, he is filled with joy, fed by his harmonious interaction with nature. The marble of the palace is like that of the lady he is pursuing. He is about to have further experiences with the ideal.

Within the palace, he is pleasantly surprised to discover a room with this description on the door: "The Chamber of Sir Anodos." He enters to find a chamber the very copy of his own, with all his peculiarly individual needs met by "invisible hands." The incident neatly points up MacDonald's emphasis upon individuality in his writings. It stands in contrast to the emphasis upon community of the Christian Socialist movement—and the thought of F. D. Maurice—which, as noted earlier, somewhat influenced MacDonald. God has made each person unique, MacDonald insists, and God intends that each maintain that uniqueness, that an individual might serve and worship the Lord in a way no one else can. The result is that people both learn and teach something of God in their relations with neighbors.

On the third day after his arrival at the palace, he finds the library and is delighted to discover that, in Fairy Land, to read a book is to become alive in the imagined world of history or fiction, or to become himself the philosopher in a book of metaphysics. In one volume he reads about a world in which children are produced not by sexual generation, but by a type of natural generation from the earth itself. As he explains the sexuality of earth to the inhabitants there, their reactions are mixed, but some long to die in order to be born into this world where they may know physical love. Though living in the Victorian Age, famous for its prudery, MacDonald does not hesitate to champion the role of sex, not as an end in itself, but as a means to a higher form of love, and hence, spiritual well-being.

Though sexual love, as distinguished from mere lust, may augment spirituality, it still falls short of what the imagination may envision as ideal love. This theme, together with that of the necessity to abandon all self-centeredness, is central to the tale of Cosmo, which

Anodos reads next in the Fairy Library. MacDonald also uses the tale to probe further his concept of the nature of art. Thus he presents the story at this juncture to counterpoint the themes we have been exploring, and to indicate more firmly how each theme eventually will be resolved.

Cosmo, a university student in old Prague, has a mirror upon his wall which periodically shows him the image of a lovely woman. Falling in love with her, he uses magic to compel her to enter his own world. She rebukes him for his use of magic, and tells him she cannot be sure of his love for her or of hers for him until they both are free from all enchantments. He must break the mirror, setting her free, though he thereby risks losing her. This he does, after a difficult inner struggle, but, in the convention of Victorian melodrama, he is wounded in the end of the tale and dies in his princess's arms.

At the point in the story when Cosmo's fascination for the princess turns to passion, MacDonald quotes, without comment, this line: "Who lives, he dies; who dies, he is alive."[6] The climax of the tale neatly works out this paradox. Cosmo must be willing to destroy the mirror and risk never seeing the princess again in order truly to have her. He must completely relinquish his power over her before they can experience love on any other but a physical level; only this renunciation, a type of spiritual death, can open to him a higher experience of life and

6. This line does not appear in the early editions; apparently MacDonald added it in a later revision (he frequently reworked his material). It appears in the 1905 edition (along with several new and fascinating illustrations by Arthur Hughes), published in London by Arthur Fifield. It also appears in the current paperback edition (Grand Rapids, Mich.: Wm. B. Eerdmans, 1964), and in that of Johannesen Printing and Publishing (1998).

love. In this manner, the two types of sensuality are
vividly illustrated in the story: the baser lust must be
renounced, in order that higher love (which, like good
dreams, is another means of grace in Fairy Land) may be
experienced.

MacDonald's doctrine of the self comes to mind,
with the emphasis that he places upon the death of the
self in his sermons on self-denial. In every phase of experience, denying indulgence in any pleasure that simply
gratifies the self gives one a higher realization of the
potential for true enjoyment inherent in that very pleasure. When Cosmo's love "withers" into passion, it becomes
mere craving for self-satisfaction, and makes the princess
a possession. To break the mirror is to give her her full
selfhood; the love she will then freely choose to give him
will be a much higher love. MacDonald will rework this
theme very often in his fiction and make it one of the
central themes of *Lilith.* To give one illustration from the
novels, this theme occurs in the sequels *Sir Gibbie* and
Donal Grant: in the first novel the shepherd-poet Donal
relinquishes the girl whom he loves to Gibbie, only to
enjoy a yet higher experience of love in the second novel.

The second theme of the Cosmo story concerns the
imperfect nature of any experience of love between the
sexes. The tale is prefaced by a direct announcement of
this idea: "Sometimes it seemed only to represent a simple story of ordinary life, perhaps almost of universal life;
wherein two souls, loving each other and longing to come
nearer, do, after all, but behold each other as in a glass
darkly." (MacDonald is echoing Paul in 1 Corinthians
13:12: "For now we see through a glass darkly; but then

face to face. . . .") The myth implies that the love relation in this life is still imperfect and will perhaps in a succeeding world be more complete. In the midst of relating Cosmo's tale, Anodos comments: "Nay, how many who love never come nearer than to behold each other as in a mirror; seem to know and yet never know the inward life; never enter the other soul; and part at last, with but the vaguest notion of the universe on the borders of which they have been hovering for years?" Cosmo's longings for his beloved can never be satisfactorily consummated so long as the mirror exists; nor can the princess be a free agent, sure of the truth of their love, until the mirror is destroyed. So, MacDonald seems to be saying, love relationships in this world fall short of perfection because of the limitations inherent in the human condition. That he sees this as universally true to human experience is probably the reason for the name Cosmo, from *cosmos*, meaning "world," and hence, universal.

The story of Cosmo also complements Anodos's quest for the marble lady. Cosmo's first fascination for the princess in the mirror is like Anodos's enthrallment with his ideal beauty in the marble block, and when his love degenerates into passion, it is like the sensual attraction Anodos felt for the Maid of the Alder. Anodos's continued pursuit of his marble lady, which is about to be resumed, will also culminate in an act of renunciation, which is for his final spiritual maturation.

DISOBEDIENCE, DESPAIR, AND DEATH

In the Hall of Statues in the Fairy Palace, Anodos again decides to summon his marble lady through song. As he sings, she gradually materializes upon a pedestal, as if an invisible veil were being lifted upward from her. Overcome by her beauty and determined to "tear her from the grasp of a visible Death," he flings his arms about her. He is immediately rebuked, for he was strongly warned upon entering the hall not to touch anything. Fleeing from his presence, his marble lady disappears through a door he is forbidden to enter. He rushes through it anyway, to find himself in a wasteland where, beside a great hole in the earth, he sits down to weep.

The Anodos who seeks to grasp his beautiful lady is not the Anodos in the grotto of the Maid of the Alder; his character has developed since then. In this instance he is prompted not by base sensuality, but by a desire to keep the lady in his sight.[7] His vision of her is of "the highest Human," which "faints away to the Divine." In his published sermons MacDonald develops the thought that when humanity becomes spiritually mature it will partake of divinity.[8] Anodos wants to retain this revelation of glory he is receiving. But the momentary vision appears only in the context of his song; to try to control it by an act of will is "in defiance of the law of the place," and he suddenly finds himself outside the palace.

Although despairing as he begins his trek through the wasteland, he makes a series of morally admirable

7. Woolf gleefully celebrates the eroticism he sees in this passage (*GK,* 80-87). Here and elsewhere he seems to overlook the way in which Anodos's spiritual and moral development is shaping his behavior.

8. "God is man, and infinitely more. Our Lord became flesh, but did not *become* man. He took on him the form of man: he was man already. And he was, is, and ever shall be divinely childlike" ("The Child in the Midst," *US I*; italics his). Cf. the ancient grandmother Irene in the Curdie stories, whose symbolic import is similar.

decisions in response to his next experiences. He is now willing to relinquish his right to his marble lady in the presence of a "better man," and he sings a little song that summarizes an important lesson he has learned:

> In thy lady's gracious eyes
> Look not thou too long;
> Else from them the glory flies,
> And thou doest her wrong.

One must allow his visions their fleeting nature, and not attempt to capture any experience in order to prolong its effects.

Death to the self is the crucial experience, the final answer to pride. This pride is stifling to his spirit. Crawling through a rocky tunnel, Anodos comes upon a gray and barren sea, the epitome of desolation. Overcome with despair, he wants to die. He walks out upon a low promontory, plunges headlong into the sea, and discovers instantaneously he has plunged into unspeakable joy. Death to the self is the final answer to pride.

References to water throughout the story are weighted with crucial significance. A stream of water flows from Anodos's bedroom into Fairy Land in the beginning of the tale, another takes him into the Fairy Palace, and a pool in a hall of the palace affords him a spiritually rejuvenating swim. Now in a sea he symbolically dies and is reborn. Water figures prominently in *Lilith* and elsewhere in MacDonald's writings. Each association with water in Anodos's adventures marks his emergence onto a higher plane of spiritual existence.

This transformation frequently occurs wherever one meets water imagery in MacDonald's works.[9]

THE BALLAD OF SIR AGLOVAILE

Anodos goes on his way, exhibiting an informed simplicity and confident childlikeness that MacDonald often associates with maturing spirituality. On an island after his sea journey, he enters a little cottage and is ministered to by a woman whom he sees as both very old and very beautiful. But the beauty that Anodos now responds to is spiritual rather than physical, residing in her eyes and voice, so that he feels a "wondrous sense of refuge and repose." Having fed him, she sings him a ballad which repeats and develops the theme found in the Cosmo story and in Anodos's adventures to this point: that, since love and desire in this life are all but inextricably allied, spiritual death into newness of life is essential in order to experience a higher love apart from base desire.

"The Ballad of Sir Aglovaile" begins with the knight Aglovaile's discovery, as he rides through the churchyard cemetery at night, of a ghost wailing a lament in the moonlight. Her song is certainly among the most charming that MacDonald ever composed:

9. In harmony with his Freudian concerns, Woolf sees Anodos achieving a return to the womb in his immersion, with water signifying "the maternal element *par excellence*" (*GK,* 69, 70). In a footnote he dismisses Jerome Hamilton Buckley's discussion of water images in *The Victorian Temper* (Cambridge: Harvard University Press, 1951), 97–105, as irrelevant to his interests (*GK,* 394, n. 17). But Buckley's discussion about the Victorians' inventive use of water symbols to suggest the spiritual new-birth is apropos. MacDonald's imagination is biblically oriented, and scripture, not Freud, is the safer guide to his meaning. See especially the use of the water-life metaphor in such apocalyptic passages as Ezekiel 47 and Revelation 22.

> Alas, how easily things go wrong!
> A sigh too much, or a kiss too long,
> And there follows a mist and a weeping rain,
> And life is never the same again.
> Alas, how hardly things go right!
> 'Tis hard to watch in a summer night,
> For the sigh will come, and the kiss will stay,
> And the summer night is a winter day.

This is the plight of the natural human condition. As the ballad illustrates, it is all but impossible to keep to the narrow path of truth and right without death to the self.

Aglovaile discovers the ghost to be that of a woman whom he once had betrayed and who had died together with his child. When he exclaims about her transformation, she replies: " 'Thou seest that Death for a woman can / Do more than knighthood for a man.' " In response to his admiration for her beauty, she invites him to come closer, but with a condition similar to the one the marble lady gave Anodos: " 'Come, if thou darest, and sit by my side; / But do not touch me, or woe will betide.' " They enjoy for a time a blissful love, but the prohibition is one that Aglovaile cannot keep for long. Awakening from a dream in which she flees, he is overjoyed to find her still by his side:

> And lo! beside him the ghost-girl shone;
>
> Shone like the light on a harbour's breast,
> Over the sea of his dream's unrest;
> Shone like the wondrous, nameless boon,
> That the heart seeks ever, night or noon:
>
> Warnings forgotten, when needed most
> He clasped to his bosom the radiant ghost.

As he takes her to himself, she turns into a corpse and disappears. Aglovaile is left only with the recurring lament which he hears "when winds are wild": "Alas, how easily things go wrong. . . ."

The simile above—the longing for the ghost-girl suggesting the spiritual longings of the human heart— should not go unnoticed. The theme of the spiritual significance of love for woman is thus given another imaginative development. Feminine beauty answers to something deep within man that is quite other than animal passion, but sensual man misreads his own spiritual longings, understanding them only in terms of physical desires. Physical love, when it is only an appropriation of the beloved for self-centered pleasure, frustrates this higher purpose; yet man in his lower stages of moral development cannot help himself. Spiritual death and rebirth is the answer, for it results in a capacity to love in an unselfish and outgoing manner. To MacDonald, the passions are essentially pure and holy, but they "go wrong" more readily than most other things. The further experiences of Anodos in the beautiful old woman's cottage continue to illustrate this point.

THE FOUR DOORS

The woman's cottage has four doors leading outward, each of which Anodos enters. Three of them lead him into environs that recall past experiences; the fourth opens into timelessness. (Both these adventures and others in the remainder of the fantasy seem to refer to MacDonald's own past.)[10] The woman tells Anodos he

10. Both Woolf (*GK,* 104) and Reis (90–91) venture some speculations about these autobiographical details. But, as Reis observes, to push such reading is unwise, and does not add to the appreciation of the literary merit of *Phantastes.*

may return to her whenever he sees her mark, a dark red cipher, upon a door. At least two of these doors lead him to experiences which echo prior themes. Songs, which now appear more frequently, begin to repeat the more basic motifs of *Phantastes*—namely, the nature of true love and the power of death.

One of the doors is labeled the "door of Sighs." Going through it, Anodos discovers he must assume second place to Sir Percival in the heart of the marble lady. (The knight is morally superior to Anodos, because he has been accomplishing good deeds while Anodos has been, up to this point, passively learning.) Anodos's noble response is to accept the situation, and to continue to love her. Returning with signs of agony to the woman of the cottage, he hears her celebrate further in song the beauty of this nobler type of love. The song concludes that it is better to express love like a well gives water, keeping itself pure and fresh by its endless giving, than to be like a cistern, growing stagnant and impure because it only receives for itself, without outlet. As noted above, this summarizes the major theme of the entire fantasy. The result of Anodos's resignation of his beloved to the knight is that he now loves her as he "had never loved her before." To serve is better than to appropriate to oneself.

After various adventures through other doors, Anodos is forced by rising waters to leave the ancient woman's cottage. Her parting advice to him is " 'Go my son, and do something worth doing.' " When Anodos previously overheard the knight and the marble lady talking about him, the knight had remarked: " 'There was something noble in him, but it was a nobleness of

thought, and not of deed.' " Clearly essential to
MacDonald's prescription for moral growth is action, the
willingness to work out in life the duties one's conscience
lays upon him by his recognition of truth.[11] Anodos's next
adventures show him nobly acting out the higher love,
the nature of which he is beginning to understand. In a
land exploited and tyrannized by three giants, he allies
himself with the ruling family to break the power of the
usurping monsters and successfully expels them.

Not all the effects of the "first worthy deed" of his
life, however, are happy ones. No sooner does he contemplate his triumph than his shadow, which forsook
him when he first entered the Fairy Palace, reappears, but
in altered form. The feelings of pride his feat nourishes
within him give rise to another severe spiritual peril.

FINAL BATTLES WITH THE SELF

Absorbed in thoughts of self-congratulation, Anodos
rides on through a forest "strangely enchanted." He is
pleased to note that his shadow is not now with him, but
he is startled to encounter a sinister-appearing knight
who is the counterpart of himself, and who he suspects is
one with the shadow. He is a "resplendent knight, of
mighty size, whose armour seemed to shine of itself,
without the sun." This knight is another of Anodos's alter
egos, possessed with a sense of self-sufficiency and inde-

11. Reis speculates that MacDonald "surely adopted" his emphasis on active
obedience from Carlyle's precept, *"Do the Duty which lies nearest thee,* which
thou knowest to be a Duty! Thy second Duty will already have become clear-
er" (41). But this seems improbable to me, given the difference between
MacDonald's tone and Carlyle's bombastic tone, the pervasiveness of this type
of insistence in MacDonald's writings, and the extent to which it is present
generally in Scripture.

pendence from God, who threatens to enslave the true Anodos. The strength of Anodos's pride has given his shadow additional substance. In spite of all his prior adventures and the moral lessons he has learned, he succumbs to the trap; pride is the easiest sin to indulge. Finding himself helpless to do anything except follow his captor, he is imprisoned in a dark, dreary tower with a single small opening high in the top. When the moon shines in upon him, Anodos feels released; when the sun's rays penetrate the tower, he feels wretched and disconsolate. A dream of his childhood innocence and shamelessness increases his longings to be freed.

These two orbs appear to symbolize aspects of God. The sun suggests God's holiness—His love that is at once burning and life-giving; the moon suggests God's beneficent providence, an expression of His grace and mercy. One can readily see how God as the sun is displeased with Anodos's imprisonment in the cell of his pride, for it cuts him off from effective service. But it is not as easy to see why the moon should conflict with the sun, seemingly fostering an illusion. Perhaps MacDonald means to indicate that even though God in His holiness is displeased with Anodos's present predicament, He does not forsake him. In spite of his present folly, God's mercy and beneficence are constantly extended to him, ready to turn this present trial to good when Anodos's humility returns.

Anodos is freed from his tower into the liberty of humility through the power of song—not his own this time, but that of another. Opening the door and emerging into the open air, Anodos is startled to find the singer to be the girl whose globe he had broken, now a woman able to sing powerfully. When he begs her forgiveness, she tells him she has nothing to forgive, because when the globe upon which she relied for song was broken, she was compelled to sing for herself—a valuable change. We recall the theme of the sacramental character of adversity developed in *At the Back of the North Wind.* This woman discovered her own talent through what seemed at the time a catastrophe. Her songs do people good, and her moral radiance is an inspiration to Anodos.

As she goes, she sings one of MacDonald's favorite songs, which appears here and elsewhere:

> Thou goest thine, and I go mine—
> Many ways we wend;
> Many days, and many ways,
> Ending in one end.
>
> Many a wrong, and its curing song;
> Many a road, and many an inn;
> Room to roam, but only one home
> For all the world to win.

To bring all men "home" is God's chief purpose and goal. In fulfilling it, He may overrule evil, creating good out of it. The very channel of His creative power is love. The very highest type of love is that which is given freely, such as that shown to Anodos by the woman/singer. Now he is about to go forth, doing deeds worth doing, motivated by his love. First, however, MacDonald reinforces the moral insights of the tale by showing Anodos, at the end of chapter 22, meditating upon what he has learned.

When he removes his armor, a symbol of pride in its subtler form, and leaves it behind, he discovers that now his shadow has completely disappeared. Its demise is simultaneous with his finally achieving selfless humility, about which he muses:

> I learned that it is better, a thousand-fold, for a proud man to fall and be humbled, than to hold up his head in his pride and fancied innocence. I learned that he that will be a hero, will barely be a man; that he that will be nothing but a doer of his work, is sure of his manhood. In nothing was my ideal lowered, or dimmed, or grown less precious; I only saw it too plainly, to set myself for a moment beside it. Indeed, my ideal soon became my life; whereas, formerly, my life had consisted in a vain attempt to behold, if not my ideal in myself, at least myself in my ideal.

Perhaps nowhere in his writings does MacDonald define more precisely the meaning of humility and the attitude of the humble man toward his ideal. Here is the fulfillment of MacDonald's epigraph to this chapter, taken from the writings of Cyril Tourneur, a dramatist contemporary of Shakespeare: "Joy's a subtil elf. / I think man's happiest when he forgets himself." Not seeing oneself in his ideal, but rather forgetting the self through absorption in the ideal, marks the narrow distinction between pride and humility.

Even so, this humility does not effect the annihilation of all false selves. Another self arises in Anodos that takes pleasure in self-degradation; this false self, too, must die. MacDonald concludes: "Self will come to life even in the slaying of self; but there is ever something deeper and stronger than it, which will emerge at last from the unknown abysses of the soul. . . ."

CONFLICTS WITH ANTAGONISTIC RELIGIOUS SYSTEMS

Anodos now undertakes further deeds "worth doing." His spiritual development, which is progressing fairly well, is a means to an end, rather than an exclusive end in itself. MacDonald emphasizes in all his writings that righteousness is nothing unless it is practically expressed in good deeds; one must become capable of performing righteous acts by the process of *doing* them. The adventures of chapter 23 show Anodos acquitting himself admirably as Sir Percival's squire.

Two episodes particularly attract attention. They illustrate the destructive effects that self-centered religious leaders and people in authority have upon sincerely seeking, childlike individuals. This knight tells Anodos that "notwithstanding the beauty of this country of Faerie . . . there is much that is wrong in it," and proceeds to relate the incident of the wooden men, which is followed by what happens inside the forest chapel.

The first incident concerns a little girl who is in search of wings to enable her to fly back to the country from which she has come. She has but to acquire them from obliging butterflies and moths, but when she asks for them, she is trampled upon by grotesque monsters "like great men, made of wood, without knee or elbow-joints, and without any noses or mouths or eyes in their faces." The knight learns that to cut down these creatures with the sword only results in more pieces that join in the attack. He finally succeeds in thwarting them by tripping them and setting them upon their heads, which renders each helpless.

The wooden men seem to represent cultic leaders. Their religious set of mind is inhuman (wooden), inflexible (without joints), and oblivious to the obvious (without noses and other sensory organs). Instead of helping the sincerely devout, who look to them to nurture the better aspects of their natures, these obtuse creatures do nothing but frustrate and hinder their spiritual aspirations. When attacked, they react by quickly producing others of similar mentality. The knight's solution—that of setting them on their heads—attempts to prove to them the intellectual shortcomings of their own system. MacDonald spent his life doing this, imaginatively in the symbolism of his fantasies and the realistic depictions of his fiction, and discursively in his sermons and essays.[12]

In the second episode, Anodos comes upon a section of the forest in which separate trails of felled trees seem to lead to a "common center." Here Anodos and the knight enter a forest chapel with walls of yew trees. Within are rows of white-robed, priestly figures reciting liturgical chants, and a large, attentive crowd. The sun has set, and darkness prevails, pierced only by starlight. Young initiates are being taken by groups of the white-robed figures to the farther end of the long chapel, where a "majestic-looking figure" is seated high upon a throne; they are then coerced into entering a door in the pedestal of the throne, where they disappear.

12. See the sermons "Jesus and His Fellow Townsmen" and "The Yoke of Jesus" (*HG*) for delineation of this religious set of mind.

The ceremony fills the knight with reverence and awe: "Incapable of evil himself, he could scarcely suspect it in another, much less in a multitude such as this." Anodos, however, his sight being "so much more keen than that of most people," suspects evil here, and, donning the robe of an initiate, makes his way to the front as though to present himself to the image on the throne. Arriving before the image, he boldly approaches and attacks it, hurling it from its seat. A "great brute, like a wolf" emerges from the chamber in the pedestal and attacks him, they struggle, and Anodos strangles the wolf. Anodos is then attacked by the indignant multitude of worshippers, and killed.

Institutionalized religion, with its strong centers of authority and more formal patterns of worship, may be symbolized here. In a manner remarkably anticipatory of twentieth-century trends, religious people appear to be exercising what MacDonald would identify as an injudicious tolerance—that of assuming all religions have a commonality in truth, inasmuch as all are expressions of the human search for the divine. Such "believers" fool the knight, but not Anodos, who actively tries to expose the emptiness of their forms of humanism, and is killed in the attempt. To expose with pure motives the error of mistaken religious attitudes is, in MacDonald's thinking, close to the most noble deed the true Christian thinker can perform.

Such exposure is necessary, but not for the sake of creedal purity. It is important to notice in each of the above episodes that it is action based upon attitudes, not creedal errors, that is being condemned. MacDonald

insists theology is not an end in itself; but rather its end
is to produce godly living. Mistaken theologies can produce zealots who brutishly attack messengers of truth.

THEMES RESOLVED

In the closing chapters of *Phantastes* MacDonald gives
final expression to the main themes that he has firmly
controlled and developed throughout the story. The first
theme concerns the nature of passion. Now "dead,"
Anodos is lamented and buried by his knight and lady.
But, far from being unconscious, he is experiencing the
bliss of a more complete life and love. That which was
coarse within him is now refined and pure: "If my passions were dead, the souls of the passions, those essential
mysteries of the spirit which had embodied themselves in
the passions, and had given to them all their glory and
wonderment, yet lived, yet glowed, with a pure, undying
fire. They rose above their vanishing earthly garments,
and disclosed themselves angels of light. But oh, how
beautiful beyond the old form!"

One is reminded of Sir Aglovaile, who mistook the
soul of his passion for its physical fulfillment, and rav-
ished the ghost-girl to his own undoing. The passions
themselves are pure. In this life they can lead one astray,
yet they are not to be despised; there is a "glory and wonderment" in them. In a future life people will not be
bereft of them, but rather they will be enabled by their
passions—then purified—to know the full blessedness of
"the land of Death." Thus MacDonald brings to
culmination the theme he has been exploring most
persistently in this fantasy.

The second theme, that of the vital role of nature in spiritual growth, also culminates in these closing chapters. *Phantastes* contains many key passages expressing this aspect of MacDonald's thinking, some of which have already been discussed.

The third theme, of the nature and power of love, is the focus of the penultimate chapter. Anodos discovers that he now is able to love others without needing to be loved in return. And he has developed a fuller knowledge of what love is:

> I knew now, that it is by loving, and not by being loved, that one can come nearest the soul of another; yea, that, where two love, it is the loving of each other, and not the being beloved by each other, that originates and perfects and assures their blessedness. I knew that love gives to him that loveth, power over any soul beloved, even if that soul know him not, bringing him inwardly close to that spirit; a power that cannot be but for good, for in proportion as selfishness intrudes, the love ceases, and the power which springs therefrom dies. Yet all love will, one day, meet with its return. All true love will, one day, behold its own image in the eyes of the beloved, and be humbly glad.

All love, including that between the sexes, is here defined. Base sensuality—any form of appropriation of another for personal satisfaction alone—destroys true love, because love is in its essence self-giving. The altruistic act of giving of oneself for the pleasure or uplifting of the beloved brings blessedness to the lover. It effects an intimacy otherwise impossible and an ability to impart good. The result is a still greater enrichment of the lover.

BACK HOME

But Anodos's "death" is not permanent. With a "pang and a terrible shudder" he finds himself transmitted back to the confines of a "more limited, even a bodily and earthly life," and he returns to his castle to assume his duties as overlord of his lands. That he is now spiritually mature is indicated by the fact that his experiences in Faerie have taken twenty-one days, and that he has lost his shadow. His chief concern is whether he can "translate the experiences of my travels there, into common life." He muses: "I have a strange feeling sometimes, that I am a ghost, sent into the world to minister to my fellow-men, or, rather, to repair the wrongs I have already done." Because he has learned selflessness and humility, Anodos can now perform these deeds with his whole heart.

Chapter 5

"*I Wis We War A' Deid!*":
Lilith

"There is no joy belonging to human nature, as God made it, that shall not be enhanced a hundredfold to the man who gives up himself—though, in so doing, he may seem to be yielding the very essence of life."

–From the sermon "Self Denial,"
Unspoken Sermons, Series Two

ALMOST THIRTY-FIVE YEARS after writing *Phantastes*, MacDonald in 1890 began *Lilith*, a fantasy for adults that he intended to be the final imaginative embodiment of his deepest beliefs. Greville records that "he was possessed by a feeling—he would hardly let me call it a conviction, I think—that it was a mandate direct from God." When Louisa MacDonald read the completed

manuscript [1] and found the imagery obscure, her distress
gave her husband "real heartache, so that he began to
question his ability to utter his last urgent message"
(*GMDW* 548). MacDonald next consulted Greville.
With his verdict that *Lilith* was the "Revelation of St.
George [MacDonald]," MacDonald overcame his
doubts, and the book appeared in final form in 1895.[2]

Since *Lilith* is more theologically based than
Phantastes, one is tempted to approach it as a theological
treatise, deciphering its assumptions. But to do so is to
diminish greatly its chief value. As a superbly crafted
myth, the reader should concentrate upon it as a story,
imaginatively participating in the adventures of the pro-
tagonist and allowing his perceptions of the eternal to
resonate with what is deepest within the heart. To do so
is to experience the impact of the central theme, that
salvation involves people becoming children of God
through willingly forsaking their "old selves" and being
transformed by grace. Closely associated with this is a
vision of the nature of spiritual liberty, the destructive
character of mere rationalism, the nature of evil, the

1. MacDonald revised the original manuscript extensively several times. Eight
manuscripts are held by the British Library (the last three are printer's copies
with minor alterations). The first five have been published in three volumes by
Johannesen Printing and Publishing in Whitethorn, CA; *Lilith: First and
Final* (1994) and *Lilith: A Variorum Edition* (1997, 2 vols. Rolland Hein, ed.).
Putting these five revisions together in a variorum edition offers a significant
look into MacDonald's creative process, together with presenting an intriguing study of his efforts to lift the narrative to the anagogic level. I calculate the
word count in the various manuscripts to be approximately as follows: MS. A,
40,000; MS. B, 93,000; MS. C, 151,000; MS. D, 144,000; and MS. E, 140,000.
The final published version contains about 96,000 words, an appreciable final
condensation.
2. Greville published *Lilith* as a centenary commemoration and included a
paraphrase of the earlier manuscript version (London: George Allen &
Unwin, 1924).

function of sorrow, and the necessity of obedience. A certain maturity of being is necessary to spiritual freedom, to understanding, and to performing any truly good deeds. All humanitarianism is vain that is not preceded by complete spiritual death to the self. Reading *Lilith* demonstrates that George MacDonald's oft-repeated desire expressed in his native Scotch, "I wis we war a' deid," held a different meaning from what at first may be supposed.

THE REGION OF SEVEN DIMENSIONS

MacDonald creates the reality of this other world and effects the transition into it with the same ease and skill that he commands in *Phantastes*. But the world of *Lilith* differs from that of *Phantastes* in that the reader has a firmer sense of "the interpenetrating yet unmingling" relationship that exists between it and our own world.[3] The hero, Mr. Vane, not only enters and returns a number of times throughout the fantasy, but Mr. Raven tells him that the two worlds are coincident and coexistent: " ' . . . you see that large tree to your left, about thirty yards away?' " he asks Vane. " 'That tree stands on the hearth of your kitchen, and grows nearly straight up its chimney.' " The hyacinths and roses growing in that world are responsible for the "peculiar sweetness" of the music coming from the piano being played in his home because they are growing coincidentally with the

3. Prickett, 223–48, argues that MacDonald's concept of two interpenetrating worlds derives from Coleridge's doctrines of the nature of the imagination and of symbol. Also, it affords a certain anticipation of Charles Williams's doctrine of coinherence, as found, for instance, in *Descent of the Dove* (1939; Grand Rapids, Mich.: Wm. B. Eerdmans, 1972).

instrument. The higher world is the anagogical level of experience, upon which the reader is made to focus full attention. That it has "seven dimensions" enhances one's fascination for its immediacy and its mystery.

The seven dimensions are formed by adding four spiritual dimensions to the familiar three. Greville credits Jakob Böhme, the seventeenth-century German mystic, with contributing to this idea, and notes that his father maintained some interest in Böhme throughout his life.[4] The image of these dimensions has not appeared in MacDonald's fantasies until now. After years of communicating his vision to the Victorian world, he had apparently concluded that a still greater emphasis needed to fall on the reality and eternal significance of the spiritual nature.

These coincidental worlds have only one common ground: morality. Mr. Raven on another occasion explains: " ' . . . most of its physical, and many of its mental laws are different from those of this world. As for moral laws, they must everywhere be fundamentally the same.' " Using moral law as a compass, readers can suspend their disbelief concerning curious psychic and material phenomena—asking only self-consistency in these areas—and depend for their bearings upon moral laws alone. When they do so they take a firmer hold upon their knowledge of moral principles, and MacDonald neatly accomplishes his purpose of intensifying the reader's moral awareness.

4. *GMDW,* 557. In his Introduction to the 1924 edition of *Lilith,* Greville explains these extra four spiritual dimensions as being "of Elemental, illimitable reach—like the four points of the compass, or the Four Elements in spiritual aspect" (xv).

MacDonald discourages speculation about the locality of this world by suggesting that it may be entered by a state of mind—a book, for instance, is one door into it. Vane overhears two shades talking: " *'Where* are we? Locality is the question! To be or not to be, is not the question.'" They are quite wrong.

ARGUMENT

The hero's name, Vane, suggests both pride and futility.[5] At the beginning of the tale, he is spiritually immature, and in Faerie he wastes a good deal of energy on well-meant but futile activities. This futility is in keeping with MacDonald's theme that actions most helpful to others can only come from those who have spiritually died to self.

The theme of the entire fantasy is that spiritual death to one's inferior selves, symbolized by sleep, is essential to being and doing. When Vane first enters Faerie and meets Mr. Raven, his initial questions have to do with where he is. But the raven counters with what is the central question of the book: " 'Tell me, then, who you are—if you happen to know. . . . Are you sure you are not your own father?—or excuse me, your own fool?'" Vane is confused to realize that he has "no grounds on which to determine" who he is. He is soon told that he is but "beginning to become an individual" and that requisite to his continued becoming is his sleeping in Eve's charnel house. Later, after he has failed to help the Little Ones and is again talking with Mr. Raven, he learns that it is necessary that he sleep before he can do anything really helpful for them, because "a man can do nothing he is not fit to do."

5. Reis suggests the meanings *vain* and *weathervane* (95).

"Sleep" symbolizes dying to one's lower selves. But it may also be seen to have another significance. Theologians have long disagreed about a perplexing question that this phenomenon raises: how is the gap filled between that state of imperfection in which the soul dies and full communion with God? Catholic theology teaches the doctrine of Purgatory, whereas Protestants tend to argue for an immediate act of God in which the soul is instantaneously transformed into the full image of Christ. MacDonald seems to combine elements of both views. The individual receives in a final long sleep in Eve's house whatever further changes are needed to travel "home to the Father."

Sleeping certainly suggests passivity, and perhaps MacDonald means to stress that these acts of dying and the process of glorification are such that the individual only needs to succumb. The act of the will is, then, all-important. To refuse to "sleep" is to retrogress on the scale of becoming. Those who refuse are under the delusion that becoming is a process of the soul making itself—that life consists of doing as they please and becoming what they choose. But those who labor under this delusion make themselves hideous entities in God's sight.

The career of Lilith illustrates all this.[6] In Mara's house on the eve of her surrendering to sleep, Lilith resists Mara's patient efforts to bring her to surrender. " 'I

6. Her name is a transliteration of the Hebrew term meaning "nightmonster." It appears only once in the Hebrew Scriptures, in Isaiah 34:14, and this in a highly poetized passage. The Jewish mystics in the Middle Ages, the Cabala, popularized her as a figure in Jewish mythology: Adam's first wife. Reis remarks that they "apparently were trying to reconcile the two different accounts of the creation of woman in Genesis" (99), Genesis 1:27 and 2:21–22, and gives a helpful exposition of the myth. Roderick F. McGillis in "George MacDonald and the Lilith Legend in the XIXth Century," *Mythlore*, 6(Winter 1979), 3–11, gives a thorough account of the history of this legend.

will be myself and not another,'" she insists. Mara counters: "'Alas, you are another now, not yourself! Will you not be your real self?'" Mara continues:

> "but another has made you, and can compel you to see what you have made yourself. You will not be able much longer to look to yourself anything but what he sees you! You will not much longer have satisfaction in the thought of yourself. At this moment you are aware of the coming change!"
>
> "No one ever made me. I defy that Power to unmake me from a free woman! You are his slave, and I defy you! You may be able to torture me—I do not know, but you shall not compel me to anything against my will!"
>
> "Such compulsion would be without value. . . ."

The primary sin here is the pride of self-sufficiency and its concomitant independence from God. The rebelling individual persists in it until he comes to the end of himself, for the evil that he has given himself to is by its very nature self-consuming. Lilith now is confronted with a free choice. What she is being compelled to is the dismissal of all illusions; only then can the will be said to be truly free. MacDonald is convinced that the soul, freed from all false selves and all false images of itself and made to realize fully the abhorrent nature of its evil acts, will repent and choose God. This is the ultimate motivating consideration behind his hope for the salvation of mankind. He is no fatalist. People are not coerced into choosing God; they will all one day simply be allowed a clear-sighted choice.[7]

---

7. See Psalm 22:25–31 and Isaiah 45:22–24 for two biblical passages that may be seen as contributing to MacDonald's view. On the biblical basis for the universalist hope, see William Barclay, *A Spiritual Autobiography* (Grand Rapids, Mich.: Wm. B. Eerdmans, 1975), 58–64. He discusses such passages as John 12:32; Romans 11:32; 1 Corinthians 15:22, 28; 1 Timothy 2:4–6; and Matthew 25:46 as supportive of his own commitment to this position.

Lilith's great delusion is that in her self-sufficiency she is free; to serve God is to be His slave, as she tells Mara above. Mara responds: "'I am no slave, for I love that light, and will with the deeper will which created mine. There is no slave but the creature that wills against its creator. Who is a slave but her who cries, "I am free," yet cannot cease to exist?'" She further tells Lilith that her exercise of power, enslaving others to her will, has been in fact the very thing to which she was herself enslaved. Mara's is a higher freedom, a freedom realized when her will grew through proper exercise to be in constant harmony with the God who created her. Such a state is the destiny of all who love the truth and are morally committed to it. Such a view of the nature of Christian liberty is essentially Augustinian.

THE WAY TO UNDERSTANDING

A certain quality of being is necessary for full understanding as well as for ultimate freedom (something Vane has not fully achieved when the fantasy closes). When Vane first enters the region of seven dimensions, he sees a radiantly beautiful bird-butterfly, and pursues it:

> A great longing awoke in me to have it in my hand. To my unspeakable delight, it began to sink toward me. Slowly at first, then swiftly it sank, growing larger as it came nearer. I felt as if the treasure of the universe were giving itself to me—put out my hand, and had it. But the instant I took it, its light went out; all was dark as pitch; a dead book with boards outspread lay cold and heavy in my hand. I threw it in the air—only to hear it fall among the heather.

In his immaturity he craves to understand by rational analysis alone; to possess a mystery is to kill it. One is reminded of Cosmo in *Phantastes,* and the fate that befell him when he attempted to possess his princess. In both stories, the hero achieves a quality of being only after dying to self. The hero's willingness to refrain from possessing a thing or a person for mere self-gratification is necessary to understanding and enjoyment.

MacDonald repeats in *Lilith* his contempt for mere rationalism that demands understanding prior to moral commitment, but at the same time he insists that the universe ultimately will be intelligible to the individual who is spiritually mature. When Vane chides Mr. Raven for talking only in riddles, Mr. Raven tells him: " 'What you call riddles are truths, and seem riddles because you are not true. . . . And you must answer the riddles. . . . They will go on asking themselves until you understand yourself. The universe is a riddle trying to get out, and you are holding your door hard against it.' " On another occasion he tells Vane: " '. . . no man understands anything; when he knows he does not understand, that is his first tottering step—not toward understanding, but toward the capability of one day understanding' "; and on still another occasion he says: " '. . . indeed the business of the universe is to make such a fool of you that you will know yourself for one, and so begin to be wise!' " The puzzling character of the universe has behind it the divine intention of creating humility and preparing people for an eventual revelation of its true nature. When people are spiritually mature enough to understand it, they will.

THE BAGS AND THE LITTLE ONES

Of especial interest in MacDonald's presentation of the theme of becoming are the Bags and the Little Ones, or Lovers. The latter apparently represent people of particularly tender sensibility and naiveté whose spiritual life is in its infancy. They owe their birth to being snatched from Bulika by the white leopardess (sorrow), who leaves them in a wood (spiritual confusion, as in Dante); there they are found by Lona (redeeming love), who takes them in her charge. But they lack the water they need to grow into maturity.

Lilith has stolen the water from the surface of their land; what remains runs underground, and seems inaccessible. The water image, similar to that in *Phantastes*, suggests life itself: the life essential. MacDonald is drawing upon the biblical image of Living Water: the life of God that Scripture indicates He bestows upon those who believe. In the conclusion of *Lilith*, "the river of the water of life" flows from around the throne of the "Ancient of Days."[8] If Vane had stayed with the Little Ones and dug them wells, Mr. Raven tells him, he would have helped them. After Vane and his party have arisen from their sleep and are journeying toward God, they find wide rivers of water restored to the land's surface. Instinctively the Little Ones plunge in and swim, and then for the first time they see "the glory of God in the limpid flow of water." A combination of Lilith's theft, Vane's misconceived philanthropy, and the Little Ones' own irresponsible attitudes has kept them from at least

8. Cf. Ezekiel 47 and John 4:10-15.

glimpsing this vision earlier, and receiving its life-giving effects.

The Little Ones' spirit of abandon and naiveté, however, does not render them immune from the danger of retrogression. When they grow apathetic and withdraw from the group, beginning to eat the fruit of the Bags, they rapidly start to become Bags. The Bags are giant creatures who are spiritually dull, cruel, and self-satisfied. Conceptually they are related to the wooden men whom the knight met and defeated in *Phantastes*. The Bags are insensitive and stupid, with a very narrow and circumscribed view of existence. They do harm to the innocent good.

One feels that here again MacDonald has one eye upon the contemporary religious scene and is commenting upon the moral and spiritual state of two types of people. The Little Ones symbolize those who have not been taught enough to be familiar with religious truth, and are therefore spiritually weak and in danger of falling away. The Bags represent those who have turned away from simple and sincere religious interests and whose lives are therefore crass and dull. The latter threaten the former, particularly when they adopt hypocritical roles. MacDonald's fiction abounds with examples.[9]

But MacDonald is not pessimistic about the outcome of the conflict between the two. Mara tells Vane that in the library of the palace at Bulika there is a manuscript in which it is written that " 'after the Lovers have gone through great troubles and learned their own name, they will fill the land, and make the giants their

9. E.g., Robert Bruce, the merchant, in *Alec Forbes of Howglen*, Rev. Slater in *Sir Gibbie*, and, in the fairy tales, the giant in "The Giant's Heart."

slaves.'" Before the Lovers, or Little Ones, leave for the siege of Bulika, they gain courage to throw off the yoke of the giants and drive them out of their land. The aggressiveness of the Little Ones in finally opposing the giants and in attacking Bulika may seem somewhat out of character with the Christian virtues of meekness, lowliness, and patience.[10] But they *are* "lovers" and their action may be meant to symbolize the power of love to overcome evil. Perhaps it is the necessity for the Christian to wage spiritual warfare—what Paul speaks of in Ephesians chapter 6—that MacDonald has in mind. In any case, their behavior is effective: they do capture Lilith.

THE BULIKANS

Similar to the Bags are the inhabitants of Bulika. They are pictured as victims of Lilith, whose cravings for power subdued them and keep them in terror, but they have developed a loyalty to her and a pride in their city. Mara describes them to Vane as a "prosperous" and "'self-satisfied people—good at bargaining and buying, good at selling and cheating . . . despising everyone they get the better of. . . . The depth of their worthlessness and height of their vainglory no one can understand who has not been there to see, who has not learned to know the miserable misgoverned and self-deceived creatures.'" No incident shows them pursuing their mercantile interests, but their inhumane attitudes toward Vane when they discover him inside their city show their low state of spiritual development.

10. See, for instance, "The Heirs of Heaven and Earth," *HG*.

In his writings MacDonald consistently directs scorn toward characters who are enslaved to money and who display the consequent vices, such as covetousness and greed. In the novel *Thomas Wingfold, Curate*, MacDonald has one of the characters, Joseph Polwarth, recite a prose poem depicting the ideal city. The means of commerce and the handling of supply and demand presented in harmony with Christian principles stand in strong contrast to the evils of this commercial "Babylon," Bulika.[11] The evil of Bulika, however, is presented rhetorically, not dramatically.

THE PRESENTATION OF EVIL

MacDonald's view of evil impacted the fictional world of *Lilith*. In *At the Back of the North Wind*, the evil of seemingly adverse circumstances and events in an individual's experience is sacramental, in that the spirit of God is able to realize spiritual good from them. But the evil of spiritually destructive attitudes is quite another thing, as he makes clear in his sermons. These attitudes, with their consequent actions, bring on a spiritual retrogression that has horrendous effects on the individual, both here and in the nether world. Such evil is the one great nightmare of the universe, enthralling large segments of mankind. Because MacDonald sees evil as negation, it is by its very nature self-destroying. The triumph of good is a necessity arising from the very nature of both good and evil.

11. MacDonald might have chosen this name to suggest "like bulk," which would underline his attitude toward the material preoccupations of the city's inhabitants. The initial "B" also recalls Babylon, the epitome of the secular world in the Book of Revelation. Reis conjectures that the name is "perhaps *bull* plus *ikon*, a pagan idol, suggesting something like Babylon" (97).

Evil will one day be seen to have been the means of realizing a far greater good than would have been possible by any other means.[12]

The imaginative presentation of these ideas in *Lilith* tends to be disappointing, because neither evil characters nor wrong decisions have much dramatic force or convincing power. The two prominent evil personages are Lilith and the Shadow. The former, who is responsible for the evil attitudes of Bulikans and the thwarted growth of the Little Ones—and consequently of the existence of the Bags—ceases to be evil with comparatively little actual suffering when she submits to sleep in Eve's charnel house. The Shadow, who seems to be a depiction of Satan, does not appear actively nefarious; he seems rather to haunt the streets of Bulika to the great danger of no one. And he, too, eventually lies down and sleeps the sleep that purifies. Thus the only final consequences of these long careers in evil is that the two will be the "last to wake in the morning of the universe."

But perhaps MacDonald's most serious failure to give convincing dramatic expression to his view of the nature of evil occurs in the experiences of Vane himself, when he disobeys Mr. Raven's explicit command that he sleep in Eve's house before he attempts to help the Little Ones. In his meeting with Mr. Raven after his initial experience with Lilith, Vane promises that he will go with him immediately to sleep. Then Vane sees the horse which will be his for his task after he awakes, and in defiance of the raven and disregard of his newly given promise, he mounts the horse and starts to ride away

12. For MacDonald's view of the nature of evil, see "The Voice of Job", *US II*.

toward the land of the Little Ones. The raven croaks: "'. . . think what you are doing! Twice already has evil befallen you—once from fear, and once from heedlessness: breach of word is far worse; it is a crime.'" When Vane refuses to be dissuaded even though Mr. Raven tells him he will do the Little Ones "other than good" if he goes through with his intention, Mr. Raven then exclaims: "'Go, then, foolish boy! . . . Take the horse, and ride to failure! May it be to humility!'"

Vane has already suffered the evil consequences of his previous mistakes: first, in the terror and physical torture that he underwent in the Evil Wood and in the captivity of the Bags; and second, in the debilitating leech bites and threat of falling under Lilith's power as her lover-cohort. As the raven points out, these experiences resulted from Vane's fear of sleeping in Eve's house and his neglect to heed the warning he was given not to trust anyone who had deceived him. These instances of evil have been comparatively plausible and appropriate to the weaknesses or mistakes to be corrected. Thus, given Vane's present presumptuous actions and the force of Mr. Raven's dire warning, one rightly expects that Vane will now be recompensed with an evil equal to his foolhardiness.

But not so. Vane marshalls the Little Ones on an expedition to Bulika. It is successful, inasmuch as Lilith is captured and delivered to Mara's house, and eventually to Eve's. The most serious cost of the siege is that Lona is killed, but her death is not really tragic, because it initiates the sleep that is necessary for her glorification. She is taken to Adam and Eve's "cemetery" where she is laid, and later she awakes with Vane and others at the "morning of the universe." Vane's grief is for no more than the loss of her companionship for the interim between her death and his own lying down to sleep. In this period, Vane develops the humility that Mr. Raven predicted would be the consequence of his disobedience: Vane asks forgiveness for his rashness and obediently fulfills the task assigned him. Punitive suffering for wrongdoing is foreign to MacDonald's system of belief; suffering for sin is exclusively corrective. But even so, to be convincing, corrective experience should have a weight that more nearly matches that of the mistake. It is difficult to see these consequences as being equal to the seriousness of Vane's disobedience.

The most satisfying scenes dealing with the nature and consequences of evil to the individual are those picturing the futile activities and empty conversations of the shades. These scenes occur before Vane meets Lilith— who oversees each scene. The first occurs as Vane passes through the Evil Wood, the place where, Mr. Raven has told him, those who refuse to sleep are burying their dead. At night Vane sees, as in a dream, "gathering multitudes" break out into tumultuous battle, filling the air with their vociferous cries. It is a battle of opposing opinions and ideological systems:

> . . . phantom-throats swelled the deafening tumult with the war cry of every opinion, bad or good, that had bred strife, injustice, cruelty in any world. The holiest words went with the most hating blow. Lie-distorted truths flew hurtling in the wind. . . . Every moment someone would turn against his comrades,

and fight more wildly than before, *The Truth! The
Truth!* still his cry.

Thus MacDonald, who would ally himself with no
system, scorns the sectarian mentality that so vehemently
expends its energies in futile clashes with those of opposing opinions. "None stooped to comfort the fallen, or
stepped wide to spare him," Vane observes, pointing up
the utter lack of humane concern that characterizes such
sectarian feuds. That they are particularly characteristic
of these beings who are extremely low on the scale of
becoming is another indication of MacDonald's low
opinion of all such activity.

Even so, these warriors are "centuries ahead" of the
two grotesque shades whose conversation Vane overhears
after he leaves Mara's cottage on the way to Bulika. They
are a man and his wife from the leisured aristocracy
whose earthly lives were characterized by sensuality and
slavish conformity to the rigid and empty social
standards of the upper-class world. Amid their bickering
and petty contentions, they are forced to help one
another: the "lord" cannot walk unless his wife binds the
joints of his skeletal knee. The raven explains their
situation to Vane:

> "My lord used to regard my lady as a worthless
> encumbrance, for he was tired of her beauty and had
> spent her money; now he needs her to cobble his
> joints for him! These changes have roots of hope in
> them. Besides, they cannot now get far away from
> each other, and they see none else of their own kind:
> they must at last grow weary of their mutual repug-
> nance, and begin to love one another! for love, not
> hate, is deepest in what Love 'loved into being.'"

These skeletons, then, are nearing the turning point
in their moral experience. It will occur when one of them
extends himself, ever so slightly, for the other. Later in
the fantasy, when the army of Little Ones is taking the
captive Lilith to Mara's house, this lord and lady again
appear. Their appreciation of the attention that the war
party gives them in passing indicates that they have
changed, repenting their former attitudes, and have
begun their long spiritual trek toward fullness of being.

As Vane observes them he wonders at the grotes-
querie of their appearance: every face is skeletal, every eye
socket is filled with a "lidless living eye" that symbolizes
their life-in-death existence. Vane speculates: "Did they
know each how they appeared to the others—a death
with living eyes? Had they used their faces, not for
communication, . . . but to appear what they wished to
appear, and conceal what they were? and, having made
their faces masks, were they therefore deprived of those
masks, and condemned to go without faces until they
repented?" In a fashion somewhat similar to Dante's
presentation of the damned in the *Inferno*, in which a
sinner's condition and punishment are appropriate to
specific sins committed on earth, MacDonald depicts
those who indulged in various forms of hypocrisy, to him
one of the most prevalent and damning of sins. Yet,
rather than being fixed in their condition (as are Dante's
sinners), MacDonald's sinners are destined eventually to
have an opportunity to repent.

The evil that befalls the damned and finally works its
own destruction in them differs only in degree from the
evil that befalls Vane. When Mr. Raven warns Vane not

to trust any person who once deceived him, Vane asks what will happen if he "forgets" the injunction. "'Then some evil that is good for you will follow'" is the reply. "'And if I remember?' Vane asks." "'Some evil that is not good for you, will not follow,'" the raven answers. This seems to indicate that Vane can only experience corrective evil. His life is constantly under the protective scrutiny of the moon, which, as in *Phantastes,* signifies the providential protection of God. That Vane sees the moon begin "to descend rolling like the nave of Fortune's wheel bowled by the gods" and disappear beyond the horizon-edge immediately after he has seized the horse and ridden off in disobedience to the raven may indicate the extent to which Vane's defiance affronts Providence itself. Nevertheless, events demonstrate that no harm befalls him except that designed to effect his good.

In MacDonald's thought, God's obligation to care for man is complete, by the very nature of both God and man. He writes in his sermon "The Voice of Job":

> God owes himself to the creature he has made in his image, for so he has made him incapable of living without him. This, his creatures' highest claim upon him, is his divinest gift to them. For the fulfilling of this their claim he has sent his son, that he may himself, the father of him and of us, follow into our hearts. . . . No claim had we to be created: that involves an absurdity; but, being made, we have claims on him who made us: our needs are our claims.

Claims upon God do not spring from any supposed human sufficiency. People are created with needs they cannot supply themselves; thus they can depend on God to supply them.[13]

God, therefore, so oversees the events of life that they are suited to minister to a person's inner state. They are designed to work upon whatever attitudes or traits need correcting. As Vane leaves Mara's house, he remarks to himself: "That which is within a man, not that which lies beyond his vision, is the main factor in what is about to befall him: the operation upon him is the event." A stronger confidence in the gracious purposes of God's involvement in the affairs of one's life could hardly be expressed.[14]

MARA AND THE LEOPARDESSES

Sorrow, like evil, is corrective. In the midst of the Evil Wood Vane finds lodging for a night in Mara's cottage. Mara is a biblical name suggesting bitterness—the soul-crushing effect of deep sorrow;[15] this enigmatic character symbolizes the sorrow that comes from severe adversity. MacDonald places a premium upon this sorrow, an importance he communicates in more than one way. Mara is, first of all, a noble character, with dignity and

13. Among others, two things follow from these "claims" that sinful man has upon God. First, the good that God would do for wayward man may well appear terrifying, and receiving it may be initially painful, as Curdie's experience with the fire of roses in *The Princess and Curdie* graphically shows. Second, God will most surely satisfy the claim of all men upon Him. It is impossible that God would be satisfied to abandon the "non-elect" to their own destinies, as the Westminster Confession asserts, the harsh declarations of which MacDonald counters in his writing.

14. MacDonald may have in mind the Psalmists' assured attitudes toward evil found in such passages as Psalm 23:4; 91:9, 10; and 121:7.

15. In the Bible, Naomi gives herself this name because "the Almighty has dealt very bitterly with me" (Ruth 1:20). Her husband and two sons had died.

beauty all her own. Few see her face, but when Vane does he finds it "lovely as a night of stars." To meet her is to encounter sorrow; to see her kind countenance is to be assured of her hidden but gracious intentions. Meeting Vane, she tells him: "'When you know me, call me by the name that seems to you to fit me. . . . That will tell me what sort you are. People do not often give me the right one. It is well when they do.'" Clearly one's attitude toward misfortune and sorrow in life indicates the true nature of his moral character.

In the fantasy Mara is associated with Psalm 30:5: "Weeping may endure for a night, but joy cometh in the morning." This is why, as she tells Vane, no one sleeps more than one night at a time in her house of sorrows; after the sleeper experiences sorrow, joy soon follows. But to try to avoid this grief or to prevent that of others, is folly. When Vane and Mr. Raven meet in the midst of Vane's experiences, and Vane suggests to him that he suspects what the Little Ones lack is water, he replies:

> "Of course it is! they have none to cry with!"
> "I would gladly have kept them from requiring any for that purpose!"
> "No doubt you would—the aim of all stupid philanthropists! Why Mr. Vane, but for the weeping in it, your world would never have become worth saving!"

Here water, which we have already suggested seems to symbolize life of spiritual quality, appears in the form of tears. Sorrow is necessary to this life: it is, it seems, the only element out of which true spiritual life grows. A philanthropy that tries only to alleviate sorrow is of questionable value, because it hinders moral growth and spiritual well-being. These ideas seem to be reinforced symbolically by the incident of the stream flowing from the spotted leopard's paw, the event beginning chapter 22. Vane sees the stream first as blood, and then discovers it has become beautiful water. The blood probably suggests suffering; the water, life.

Both Mara and Lilith have a cat, or leopardess self, and both bear a close relation to the Shadow. Vane finds it difficult at first to tell the two apart, beyond the fact that the one leopardess has spots while the other is pure white. He knows that Lilith is the spotted leopardess because its actions are consistent with her character. But he is puzzled at first by the actions of the white leopardess, who is closely associated with the Shadow, frequently seen following at his heels. Vane eventually discovers, however, that the white leopardess means to befriend him. When Vane begins to follow the Shadow, she drives him back; when Lilith tries to seduce him, she gives a warning cry; and when he is spending a night alone in the streets, she warms and comforts him. Perhaps MacDonald is showing his reader that, although sorrow is associated with evil, it protects the individual who heeds its warnings from being really harmed by it— that is, sorrow leads to salvation. The spotted leopardess, on the other hand, is truly dangerous. It is this one that inflicts the leechlike bites on Vane in an attack which, if repeated, would have killed him, and whose snatching of children is deadly.

Vane further learns that the white leopardess steals the babies to keep them alive, not to kill them. Also, when the two leopardesses fight, the white has the "greater endurance" and prevails. Clearly, the presence of the white leopardess in Bulika acts as a restraining force, stemming the power and controlling the effects of evil. In this way MacDonald may be symbolically expressing Paul's observation: "For godly grief produces a repentance that leads to salvation and brings no regret, but worldly grief produces death" (2 Cor. 7:10).

BIBLICAL SOURCES OF SYMBOLS

The reader is reminded of a number of Scripture passages when reading *Lilith*, and many of the book's symbols are similar to scriptural ones. These symbols include references to childbearing being the death (and salvation) of Lilith (cf. 1 Tim. 2: 15); new names and knowing one's name (cf. Rev. 2:17); going "in and out" of home (cf. John 10:9); the "dead burying their dead" in the Evil Wood (Matt. 8:22); the shades' comment to Lilith, " 'Thou wilt soon become like unto us' " (Isa. 14:9, 10); "the mirror of the Law of Liberty" into which Lilith looks (cf. Jas. 1:22-25);[16] the Shadow's head under Eve's heel (cf. Gen. 3: 15); removing the beam from one's eye (Matt. 7:3-5); and various aspects of the universe at the time of its "morning" (cf. Rev. 21, 22). Two other important symbols whose significance may be defined in terms of biblical

16. Woolf finds this a "confused and confusing" image (*GK,* 363), but a comparison of MacDonald's use of this image with its source in James makes the meaning clear enough. Cf.: "Nothing is so pleasant to ordinary human nature as to know itself by its reflection from others. When it turns from these warped and broken mirrors to seek its reflection in the divine thought, then it is redeemed; then it beholds itself in the perfect law of liberty" (*The Marquis of Lossie,* chapter 2). This suggests Lilith's experience with mirrors throughout the fantasy. The liberty Lilith knows in the end is that higher liberty in goodness that Mara explained to her when she was brought, bound, to her dwelling.

passages must be considered more fully: Lilith's dark spot and her closed hand.

From Lilith's first introduction into the fantasy, she is identified as the woman with the spot on her side. In her struggles in Mara's cottage just before she is sent a vision of her true self as God sees her, a worm appears and enters her being through a spot, now grown quite large. As one recalls, Lilith is the leopard with the spots. In scriptural symbolism, spots suggest blemishes and are often associated with sin. In Levitical law, for instance, a sacrifice to God must be without spot. A quotation from Jeremiah is particularly germane: "Can the Ethiopian change his skin or the leopard his spots? Then also you can do good who are accustomed to do evil" (13:23). Gangrene, a spot that quickly spreads, is in the English of the King James Version called a "canker," which suggests cankerworm. Christ often characterized hell as the place where "their worm does not die, and the fire is not quenched" (Mark 9:48).

In describing Lilith's spot, MacDonald seems to have all this in mind, together with his hope for the final salvation of man. The leopard may not be able to change its spots, but the spots may change it. The growing spot seems to suggest evil eating like a canker to the very quick of Lilith's being, destroying all but her very essence, which then can submit to the sleep that heals and makes whole. The worm proceeds out of the fire on Mara's hearth, and is itself described as "white hot, vivid as incandescent silver, the live heart of essential fire." As the worm penetrates into Lilith's being, she has the terrible experience of "seeing herself." Mara explains:

"She is far away from us, afar in the hell of her self-consciousness. The central fire of the universe is radiating into her the knowledge of good and evil, the knowledge of what she is. She sees at last the good she is not, the evil she is. She knows that she is herself the fire in which she is burning, but she does not know that the Light of Life is the heart of that fire."

Apparently MacDonald is interpreting Christ's imagery of worm and fire. The irreducible essence of man is itself a fire, as is the holy nature of God, capable of consuming all that is foreign to it. This scene appears to be a definitive depiction of MacDonald's view of human nature and the meaning of human sinfulness.

The meaning of the symbol of the clenched hand may derive from this same warning Christ gives concerning hell. He admonishes: "And if your hand causes you to sin, cut it off; it is better for you to enter life maimed than with two hands to go to hell, . . ." (Mark 9:43). Lilith's left hand has been clenched throughout the story, and becomes the focus of attention in Mara's cottage when it is the final remaining obstacle that keeps her from sleep. She protests that she is unable to open it and finally asks Adam to cut it off. He does, using a sword that brings "healing and not hurt." She then immediately falls asleep.

The clenched hand seems to suggest Lilith's acquisitive nature, her taking and keeping things from others. Her yielding her hand suggests her willingness to restore what she has taken. Vane's burying her severed hand restores water to the land, which recalls her original stealing of the water from the Little Ones. But the

principle governing her life has been taking from others
what is rightfully theirs in order to have power over
them. Mr. Raven describes her to Vane as living "by the
blood and lives and souls of men." Her acquisitiveness, so
deeply embedded within her that she cannot free herself
from it, seems to be the "offending member" from which
she must be freed to "enter into life."

SALVATION THROUGH CHILDBEARING

The prophecies that Lilith has feared throughout the
story are that her child shall be the death of her and that
she "shall be saved by her childbearing." The manner in
which this occurs in the fantasy may be taken to represent MacDonald's view of the meaning of the Old
Testament assertion that God in his jealousy visits the
iniquities of the fathers (mothers?) upon the children. If
God punishes sin, MacDonald insists, it is solely for the
sake of destroying the sin and saving the sinner: if God
visits suffering upon children for the sake of their parents, it must be necessary for the salvation of both.[17] The

17. See, for instance, Deuteronomy 5:9. On punishment, MacDonald writes:
"When a man loathes himself, he has begun to be saved. Punishment tends to
this result. Not for its own sake, not as a make-up for sin, not for divine
revenge—horrible words—not for any satisfaction to justice, can punishment
exist. Punishment is for the sake of amendment and atonement. God is bound
by his love to punish sin in order to deliver his creature: he is bound by his justice to destroy sin in his creature" ("Justice," *US III*). Commenting on Luke
4:16–21, MacDonald says this about vengeance: "The point at which the Lord
stops in his reading is suggestive: he closes the book, leaving the words 'and the
day of vengeance of our God,' . . . unread: God's vengeance is as holy a thing
as his love, yea, is love . . . but, apparently, the Lord would not give the word a
place in his announcement of his mission: his hearers would not recognize it
as a form of the Father's love, but as vengeance on their enemies, not
vengeance on the selfishness of those who would not be their brother's keeper"
("Jesus and His Fellow Townsmen," *HG*).

pattern of events involving Lilith and Lona illustrates this belief.

As Adam's first wife, Lilith bears him Lona and then, supposing that she had herself created the child, wants Adam to worship her. When he refuses and she flees to become queen of Hell, she begins to suppose that parents lose their immortality in their children, and sets out to destroy Lona (thus symbolizing selfishness). But Lona grows up to become the epitome of love, and the loving child desires the redemption of the parent.

With her army of Little Ones, Lona pursues Lilith to Bulika, and at their meeting runs to embrace her. Lilith kills her daughter: the evil parent suffers in hate, the good child in love. But immediately the Little Ones—offspring, as it were, of Lona's love—overcome Lilith and take her to her "death" in Eve's house. The prophecies are fulfilled in the redemption of each.

PRACTICAL ATONEMENT

The reconciling of the world to God has been effected in Christ, but reconciliation—or practical atonement— must be made between people who have offended each other. When Lilith is about to succumb to sleep in Eve's house, Eve tells her: " 'Your own daughter you have but sent into the loveliest sleep, for she was already a long time dead when you slew her. And now Death shall be the atonemaker; you shall sleep together.' " Death to lower selves is prerequisite to all effective altruism; hence, we are told, Lona had previously died. Her previous deaths are, of course, phenomena quite distinct from her

physical death at Lilith's hands.[18] In Eve's house Lilith's
enmities toward Lona will be replaced with loving
attitudes as they sleep together; thus, practical atonement
will be realized.

This practical atoning for past wrongs is not to be
taken as a substitute in MacDonald's thought for the
Atonement of Christ. Christ's death brings God and
men together by revealing God's love, which offers
forgiveness to all men for all sin. The estrangement
between God and the world is bridged by Christ's death.
All lesser estrangements between people must be worked
out among themselves. God is concerned with making
people become righteous—not simply declaring them to
be so by imputing righteousness to them—and an
essential part of this process is their working to right the
wrongs they have committed. After Vane succumbs to
sleep (during which he dreams), he recounts: "Then, of a
sudden, but not once troubling my conscious bliss, all the
wrongs I had ever done, from far beyond my earthly
memory down to the present moment, were with me.
Fully in every wrong lived the conscious I, confessing,
abjuring, lamenting the deed, making atonement with
each person I had injured, hurt, or offended." This scene
brings to mind one of MacDonald's favorite texts, words
of Christ that recur in his sermons: "Truly, I say to you,

18. Failing to allow MacDonald the twofold sense of death as both physical
and spiritual, Woolf is quite unhappy with this passage (*GK,* 363). That Lona
formerly had died to her lower selves is evidenced by her selfless serving of the
Little Ones (without such death, MacDonald has told us, philanthropy is inef-
fective). Sleep in Eve's cemetery—still necessary—follows at the proper time.
Lilith had killed Lona physically, which is quite another matter, and she is
rightfully to blame for doing so.

you will never get out till you have paid the last penny"
(Matt. 5:36).[19]

DREAMING OR AWAKE?

Despite his progress, Vane has not yet reached perfection. He is beset by doubts, wondering if it is all simply a
lovely but deluding dream. "'Be content for a while not
to know surely,'" Father Adam replies. "'The hour will
come, and that ere long, when, being true, thou shalt
behold the very truth, and doubt will be for ever dead.'"
The essential thing, Father Adam tells Vane, is to never
waver in obedience to the truth he knows. "'Trials yet
await thee, heavy, of a nature thou knowest not now,'" he
warns. Thus MacDonald conveys imaginatively a feeling
for the degree of spiritual development Vane must still
undergo to "look Truth in the face."

In his sermons MacDonald presents the end of his
vision as full, active, loving fellowship between perfected
humanity and the Triune God, but he stops short of
attempting to project this imaginatively in *Lilith*.[20] He is
careful, rather, to maintain the dynamic sense of move-

19. Because of this insistence on the practical aspects of atonement, some readers may misunderstand MacDonald's position. He explains: "I believe that
Jesus Christ is our atonement; that through him we are reconciled to, made
one with God. There is not one word in the New Testament about reconciling
God to us. . . . It is God who has sacrificed his own Son to us; there was no
way else of getting the gift of himself into our hearts. Jesus sacrificed himself
to his Father and the children to bring them together—all the love on the side
of the Father and the Son, all the selfishness on the side of the children. . . .
Who that believes in Jesus does not long to atone to his brother for the injury
he has done him?" ("Justice," *US III*). He opposes any theory of the Atonement
that leaves man solely the passive recipient of its effects.
20. See particularly "The Creation in Christ," *US III*.

ment ever upward into increasingly lovely states of more complete life. "'The Life keeps generating ours,'" Lona explains. "'. . . here all is upwardness and love and gladness.'" In avoiding the suggestion of stasis that one encounters in Dante's paradise and insisting instead upon continual growth and development, MacDonald manifests his own romantic temperament and reminds us again how much he belongs to the romantic spirit of his age. Vane continues to grow, depicted as experiencing an everincreasing unity with all things:

> A wondrous change had passed upon the world—or was it not rather that a change more marvellous had taken place in us? . . . Every growing thing showed me, by its shape and colour, its indwelling idea. . . . The world and my being, its life and mine,were one. The microcosm and macrocosm were at length atoned, at length in harmony! I lived in everything; everything entered and lived in me.

The quest for one's home, with which the fantasy began, is nearing fulfillment as Vane's capacity to receive the sacramental energies of the universe becomes more complete. As Vane's feelings of estrangement from and bewilderment with the universe are diminishing, his individuality and personhood are growing. He is not losing himself in the All.

The essential sacrament for the continuance of this development seems to be still more lovely dreams; to "awake" to the surface realities of the actual world seems to be a retrogression. Vane is "alone, in the land of dreams."

When he wishes himself awake, he tumbles back
into this world, and feels "unspeakable despair." He
blames himself because he had fled his dream.
Apparently one should, for his spiritual health, maintain
the strength of his best dreams, but one cannot always
summon them at will. Vane futilely attempts to return to
Father Adam's realm. Then he suddenly awakes on his
couch in Eve's house, with Lona by his side, and realizes
that he had never lost her. For MacDonald doubts and
moods of seeming spiritual emptiness were not an
unusual part of his spiritual odyssey. He seems to be suggesting here that although the good dream may not stay
in constant focus, it does recur. Also, the distinctions
between states of consciousness imaged by waking and
sleeping become unimportant, and MacDonald finalizes
his point that in this upward progression of spiritual
development each prior state becomes like a past dream,
with each new state being one of more intense
consciousness.

At the conclusion of the penultimate chapter, just as
Vane and his party are at last approaching the throne of
"the Ancient of Days" and in a cloud of glory are lead by
a "hand, warm and strong," through a door with a golden
lock, Vane suddenly finds himself "alone in his library,"
and faces again the question, Is it all illusion? But the
answer issues from the lips of Hope, that, although the
dream came from Vane's own "dark self," it was put there
by God, by whose integrity it will be realized. He therefore affirms: "But when I wake at last into that life
which, as a mother her child, carries this life in its
bosom, I shall know that I wake, and shall doubt no

more." For this, Vane is content to wait—and, it would
seem, so was MacDonald.[21]

EVALUATION

Within MacDonald's system of thought, all must do as
Lilith has done to be saved. The sooner an individual
earnestly undertakes to die to his inferior selves, and to
nurture his true self, the sooner he comes to spiritual
health and growth. For those who will not do so, there
are experiences of constantly increasing pain and horror
ahead. Lilith makes us feel this view of the nature of salvation with an imaginative power wielded by few pieces
of literature dealing with the eternal destiny of the world.

Nevertheless, the fantasy as a whole is an uneven
performance in its final form, and somewhat inferior to
Phantastes. One cannot help feeling that the original
version could have been revised into a more aesthetically
satisfying fantasy. The first version is more compact, contains less overt sermonizing, and omits the material that
is least well-realized dramatically: Lona, the Little Ones,
the Bags, and the entire incident of Vane's disobedience
to Adam.[22] MacDonald's actual revision on the whole
dilutes the material, and although it is still generally far

21. I find no basis in *Lilith* or in MacDonald's writings in general to agree
with Woolf's harsh assessment: "Close reading of *Lilith* has convinced me . . .
that, despite powerful and occasionally moving passages, it is feeble, ambigu-
ous, and inconsistent in its imagery, full of senile hatreds and resentments, and
the most violent in its aggressions of all MacDonald's works. The consolations
that it professes seem to have lost their meaning for the author himself" (*GK,*
332). Reis disagrees, contending that the ending of *Lilith* is consistent with
MacDonald's affirmation of both life and death, and with his view that
enlightenment in this life is never complete (102).

22. Greville opines: "Comparing carefully the two versions, some will think
the earlier a better and simpler narrative" (*GMDW,* 548). After reading the earlier version, I agree.

from allegory (in the sense of a very transparent and mechanical one-to-one relation of meaning to symbol), the final version does take some steps in that direction. Perhaps here is another evidence of MacDonald's romantic temperament: material that stands closest to the original creative vision retains more of the original fire; alterations tend to diminish the flame.

Positively, *Lilith* is to be credited with having generally vivid characters—for myth—and a rather vivid sense of place. MacDonald handles the transitions between the two worlds with expertise. The aura of the dream, with the startling immediacy of its scenes and the peculiar force of its logic, is maintained with admirable consistency. In addition, much of the symbolism serves MacDonald's ideological purposes with an impressive strength. But, these qualities acknowledged, the weaknesses remain to disappoint: the weight of idea that is not integrated with the symbolism, the generally weak dramatic quality, and the lack of convincing moral growth within Vane himself.

Chapter 6

"If You Would But Write Novels, Mr. MacDonald"

"This made it more likely that he had seen a true vision; for instead of making common things look commonplace, as a false vision would have done, it had made common things disclose the wonderful that was in them."

—"The Shadows"

LILITH WAS WRITTEN AFTER MACDONALD spent over thirty years detailing his vision of the meaning and significance of life in his many long novels. The novels are impressive in the degree to which they achieve a satisfying artistic integration of his faith with the demands of literary conventions. In a warm and fascinating essay written as a tribute to his father, MacDonald's son Ronald relates this incident:

149

Once I asked him why he did not, for a change and
variety, write a story of mere human passion and artistic plot. He replied that he would like to write it. I
asked him then further whether his highest literary
quality was not in a measure injured by what must to
many seem the monotony of his theme—referring to
the novels alone. He admitted that this was possible;
and went on to tell me that, having begun to do his
work as a Congregational minister, and having been
driven . . . into giving up that professional pulpit, he
was no less impelled than compelled to use unceas-
ingly the new platform whence he had found that his
voice could carry so far.[1]

George MacDonald was first of all a Christian;
secondly, an artist. As mentioned in the opening chapter,
he turned from writing fantasy and poetry to writing
novels early in his career because he saw the novel as an
effective medium for his message, and because his
publisher urged him to do so.

Had MacDonald's conscience not compelled him to
communicate his message to a world he perceived to be
in great need, he perhaps would have written few—if
any—novels. No doubt he would have made more
contributions to literature in the genre he liked best:
fantasy. But, as it was, he was driven to make as clear as
he could to as large an audience as possible his understanding of the relation of Christian truth to human
experience. The great popularity of the novel form—

1. "George MacDonald: A Personal Memoir," *From a Northern Window*
(London: Nisbet, 1911). 66–67. This collection of essays lists no editor; Ian
Maclaren writes the first. Reis, also quoting this passage, comments: "Scarcely
any other writer of fiction in any literature so consciously regarded his function to be that of a teacher and preacher, rather than to be that of an enter-
tainer, artist, or money-earner" (47).

Dickens, Thackeray, and Trollope were in vogue at the time—must have seemed to offer him the opportunity he wanted.

Although MacDonald was not unmindful of the distinct literary conventions that govern the separate genres of myth and the realist novels, in his novels the distance between them is less than one might suppose. He combines them by creating an awareness of the duality of levels in life—the commonplace and the ana-gogic—and keeping the readers' attention focused upon the relationship between these. Through the dynamic of myth he stimulates desire to discern moral beauty. At the beginning of *What's Mine's Mine*, he describes the ideal reader as one "whose heart, not merely his eye, mirrors what he sees—one who not merely beholds the outward show of things, but catches a glimpse of the soul that looks out of them, whose garment and revelation they are." His discerning fictional characters see this "soul" as permeating existence, so the value of the commonplace lies in its potential to become spiritually significant, to show that "all ugliness, that is not evil, is undevelopment." Dramatic interest is generated by characters that develop from spiritual ugliness to beauty.

Careful to keep this concern in focus as his stories develop, MacDonald excels in realistic scenes that suggest their spiritual dimensions. Stilted though his plots may be at times, invariably some characters are keenly concerned with the anagogic level of life, aptly discerning and explaining how life may be lifted to this height. They are shown as standing in harmony with the true nature of things—the grace endemic in their world—rather than standing over against their world, as characters created by authors with Christian purposes too often do. This is not to say MacDonald does not see the world as fallen, but he also sees a world endued with grace.

The blending of these levels is especially effective in MacDonald's Scottish novels, works which should be read in their unabridged and "untranslated" editions. The slight effort necessary to master the Scottish language of the conversations rewards the diligent reader. (A "Glossary of Scottish Terms" is appended to this book.) These conversations, which often combine an aura of mythic otherness with a colloquial intimacy, present the author at his creative best. On the level of realism they do much to establish MacDonald's stature as a forerunner of the so-called "kailyard school" of Scottish novelists— those who graphically depict the quainter aspects of peasant life.

MacDonald must have been attracted to the writing of myth at the beginning of his long career because he saw the potential it had to assert the presence of this transcendent yet immanent reality and to explore the moral imperatives it places upon the lives of people. When writing novels became for him a necessary alternative to writing fantasies, his purposes did not change; they simply became more directly and explicitly revealed. In the novels, symbolic embodiment tends to give way to illustration in the lives of characters that appear as real people. In contrast to the other realist authors of the time, MacDonald focused on the elusive yet pervading realities by which the destinies of people are shaped. He also is quite distinct from such a contemporary moralist as George Eliot, whose frequent observations on the moral qualities of her characters serve to reveal character itself and the effects of human behavior upon society, rather than to assert man's immortality and the effects of his behavior upon his eternal destiny. Several other religious novelists were writing at the same time as MacDonald; but few, if any, were as prolific as he, nor do their works seem to achieve as satisfying an integration of the eternal with the temporal as his do.

The novel as a literary type is an attempt to picture daily human experience. For the imaginative and conscientious Christian author, the novel can become a sort of gauge for measuring the validity of his understanding of Christian truth in its practical reaches. Inadequate views of what Christianity consists of and means can be offensive to the discerning reader's sense of reality. Thus the Christian who would write a viable novel is pressured by the very nature of his medium to develop a valid view of the relation of Christian idea to life.

Writing novels did work to keep MacDonald's faith practical and psychologically apt, but this is not to say he wrote great novels. True, the imagined world his novels project is peopled by a startling number of believable characters reacting to experiences in ways that offer deft insight into human behavior. But his plots tend to be conventional, predictable, and melodramatic—a lamentable flaw.

A factor contributing to poor quality is the pace at which MacDonald wrote: he was a very energetic author who produced an astounding amount of material. Greville lists sixty titles in his bibliography of his father's works, and he quotes Ronald as saying that twenty-five of them are novels.[2] It is undeniable that MacDonald possessed the gift of telling a story with verve and intrigue, and portions of his work are artistically admirable. However, both his haste and fatigue are too often evident.

Archetypal patterns and images form a firm substructure in both MacDonald's fantasies and his novels.[3] To note some of the more outstanding ones offers us a convenient way of seeing all of the novels in relation to each other as well as to the fantasies, and underscores MacDonald's mythic bent.

Several archetypal images are prominent in both the novels and the fantasies: 1) the journey, during which the hero comes into a higher state of moral and spiritual being through a series of related episodes; 2) the sage or prophetess, who gives necessary counsel and advice along the way; 3) the wasteland, through which the hero moves to self-knowledge; 4) the poet, whose powers of vision discern the spiritual world and whose songs move both himself and his listeners toward it, and 5) the ideal woman, who inspires others toward a fuller knowledge of the Ideal. Each of these archetypes bears a particularly close relation to MacDonald's concept of becoming and is used to show how the individual moves toward spiritual maturity.

2. *GMDW,* 563. There are at least this many. Woolf counts 25 (*GK,* 4); Reis arrives at 29 (28). The exact number one reaches depends upon whether he includes as novels some of the shorter works MacDonald designated as "tales," and also whether he includes novels intended for adolescents, such as *Gutta Percha Willie: The Working Genius.*

3. Reis discerns Jungian archetypal patterns in character and plot. See his chapter "The Symbolic Muse."

THE JOURNEY

The image of the journey, which is prominent in the fantasies, appears both literally and symbolically in the novels. In the fantasies, both Anodos and Vane journey through Faerie, experiencing the various adventures of the story. In the novels, the characters most often make spiritual journeys, so that the archetype of the journey appears as the spiritual road they travel in the process of their moral development. At the beginning of many novels, the hero or heroine has certain character flaws that indicate the distance he or she has to travel on the road to inner maturity. The incidents of the novel then shape and nurture this development, so that by the end the character has arrived at his or her spiritual destination. *Guild Court* (1868) is a typical example, also illustrative of other characteristics of MacDonald's fiction.

The plot provides the challenges which Thomas Worboise, the hero, must face along his spiritual journey. At the beginning of the novel, Tom is self-centered, ambitious for the "good life" of materialism, indecisive, and rather frivolous, although these traits are not so strong that they alienate the reader from him. He is the son of a shrewd, ambitious lawyer and an invalid mother of strong evangelical persuasion, and he is working as an apprentice clerk to his father's friend, Mr. Boxall.

Tom is secretly meeting Lucy Burton, an admirable and attractive but poverty-stricken girl who lives with her grandmother Boxall, mother of Tom's employer. His father, however, wants his son to court one of Boxall's own daughters, Mary, because such an alliance would put him into position to inherit the business. The self-indulgent manner in which Tom behaves toward these girls, both of whom love him, underscores the unpleasant qualities of his character. But, forced to decide between them, he chooses Lucy, falling out of favor with the Boxalls.

Boxall makes out his will with the help of Lawyer Worboise, and in a moment of carelessness, he names his lawyer his beneficiary should his wife and daughters die. Ironically, no sooner does Boxall do this than he and his family are shipwrecked while taking a vacation, and all die in the disaster. Eager for wealth, Worboise presses his claim, even to the extent of cruelly evicting Lucy and her grandmother from their apartment above the premises.

Meanwhile, Tom begins the journey that brings him to spiritual enlightenment. He falls under the influence of a German language instructor who exercises an evil power over him and draws him into gambling. Ruined, dejected, and filled with shame, Tom, having stolen money from the Boxall business to pay a gambling debt, leaves home. His spiritual journey is now symbolized by his physical journey. After a series of adventures in which he rescues a child from drowning and goes to sea as a sailor, he determines to return to Guild Court (a particular small court in London in which small shops and Boxall's business are located and the minor characters live) and ask Lucy's forgiveness.

Doing so, he comes into contact with a Mr. Fuller, an unconventional clergyman who conducts his own nightly church and is identified as being somewhat "Broad Church" in his theology. Mr. Fuller convinces Tom of the necessity of making restitution to those whom he has wronged. Tom does so with admirable courage, his experiences having brought him to his senses, and Lucy is joyously reconciled with him. In the end, Tom is instrumental in proving that since the Boxall family did not all die at the same time (a daughter survived her parents for a short time), the business in question cannot legally go to his father. In the meanwhile, he is reconciled with his father, who comes to admire him for his courage and determination.

When in utter dejection Tom has his conversation with Mr. Fuller, the clergyman philosophizes about Tom's past experiences in a manner that reveals MacDonald's intention in presenting the spiritual journey:

> "You are more honorable now than you were before. Then you were capable of the crime; now, I trust, you are not. It was far better that, seeing your character was such that you could do it, you should thus be humbled by disgracing yourself than that you should have gone on holding up a proud head in the world, with such a deceitful hollow of weakness in your heart. It is the kindest thing God can do for his children, sometimes, to let them fall in the mire. You would not hold by your Father's hand; you struggled to pull it away; he let it go, and there you lay. Now that you stretch forth the hand to him again, he will take you, and clean, not your garments only, but your heart, and soul, and consciousness."

The journey with its harsh experiences is necessary, because it produces virtue. The pain and disgrace that are inevitable upon the journey—all external evils—are justified because they are intended to humble and enlighten the sufferer. They are meted out by a loving Father who wants to chastise His child in order to turn him to righteousness. Wearied by the episodes of the journey, the defeated individual turns in weakness to God, who both renews him and, in the future, responds to his obedience by giving the power to grow. Thus the journey image accomplishes the same ends in the novels as it does in the fantasies.

An interesting variation of the journey motif in MacDonald's novels occurs when he traces the growth of children to both physical and spiritual maturity. In an earlier novel, *Alec Forbes of Howglen* (1865)—which remains in many ways the most delightful of the novels— MacDonald discovered his ability to draw children convincingly. Apparently he also discovered in this novel that tracing the physical growth of an individual, particularly as he undergoes hardships in childhood, can be a fitting and helpful corollary of spiritual development. In fact, many of MacDonald's novels may be classed as bildungsroman: the journey image acquires the dimension of traveling through life toward adulthood as well as traveling through adult experience toward spiritual maturity.

Little Annie Anderson in *Alec Forbes of Howglen* is a convincing and memorable character. An unwanted orphan, she lives in the deprived and niggardly atmosphere of the home of her "benefactor," Robert Bruce, a skinflint grocer. The scene of Annie in her barren garret room at night, deathly frightened by the rats and crying out in prayer, " 'O God, tak care o' me frae the rottans,' " makes a lasting impression upon the reader. In its vivid and pathetic portrayal it is not unlike a passage from Dickens.

As a child Annie deeply admires Alec Forbes, slightly older than she. This admiration blossoms into a worshipful love as he protects her from bullying school-mates and a tyrannical schoolmaster. Annie grows toward spiritual maturity early in her life, her nature being purged of its dross by unusually severe—but convincing—childhood hardships. Alec, however, must go off to college, start drinking, visit a brothel, and finally go to sea before he realizes how lost he is. He then undergoes a type of conversion that brings him to his senses and prompts his return to home and Annie. This version of the journey archetype later becomes the pattern for several of MacDonald's more successful novels, such as *Robert Falconer, Wilfrid Cumbermede,* and *Sir Gibbie.*

In many of the novels the chief deterrent to a successful journey toward spiritual maturity is contact with false ideas about God's character and manner of working in the world, particularly those fostered by the mean and narrow popular versions of Calvinist doctrines. Many heroes are genuinely perplexed by the doctrines preached by dissenting evangelical groups. A case in point is the consternation little Annie Anderson feels when she attends the "missionar-kirk" and hears a sermon on the doctrine of election. The scenes in *Malcolm* of the revival meeting in a cave present another travesty of true religious experience: the congregation is seized by fits of emotional frenzy. MacDonald's sense of indignation at the error and vulgarity of such religious expressions is very strong. He distinguishes between them and his sense of the truth with scathing rebuke.

Many of his portraits of evangelical believers enslaved to rigid Calvinist doctrines are memorable. Mrs. Worboise, Tom's mother in *Guild Court*, is a good study of the morally despicable attitudes that such a commitment can generate. She is an invalid, constantly ministered to by Mr. Simon, a dissenting minister; together the two of them keep her husband and almost keep Tom from entering the kingdom of heaven. MacDonald describes them caustically:

> She and her priest belonged to a class more numerous than many of my readers would easily believe, a great part of whose religion consists in arrogating to them-selves exclusive privileges and another great part in defending their supposed rights from the intrusion of others. The thing does not look such to them, of course, but the repulsiveness of their behaviour to those who cannot use the same religious phrases, indicating the non-adoption of their particular creed, compels others so to conclude concerning their religion. . . . Alas for that people! whose god is paltry, shallow-minded and full of party spirit; who sticks to a thing because he has said it, accepts a man because of his assent, and condemns him because of his opinions. . . .

Mrs. Worboise has a compulsive desire to save her son's soul, a wish that he undergo a conversion according to the exact steps she would prescribe. But her obsession only oppresses Tom, alienating him from her and keeping him from a true experience of God.

Mr. Fuller, the maverick clergyman, helps Tom develop a genuine knowledge of God by explaining his need to approach God personally and sincerely. Tom is told he must first of all make restitution for the wrongs he has done and then exercise an obedient faith: " 'You must give yourself up to the obedience of his Son entirely and utterly, leaving your salvation to him, troubling yourself nothing about that, but ever seeking to see things as he sees them, and to do things as he would have them done. And for this purpose you must study your New Testament in particular. . . !' " This effort to bring one's view of life into conformity with God's will and commands is clearly distinct from a more narrowly prescribed insistence upon accepting a "plan of salvation." It does not rely upon a mechanical handling of biblical "proof texts" and an emotional conversion.

Although MacDonald's opposition to what he views as perversions of true Christian thought at times appears to be labored, he also pays large tribute to those staunch characters, particularly Scottish, whose rigid evangelical commitment to stern Calvinist doctrine makes them Christians of sterling virtue. Old Thomas Crann in *Alec Forbes of Howglen* and Mrs. Falconer, Robert's devout grandmother in *Robert Falconer*, are two good examples of such admirable characters. MacDonald muses in *Malcolm*, "Calvinism itself has produced as loving children as abject slaves, with a good many between partaking of the character of both kinds," and he does make an objective attempt to draw both kinds of believers in his works. But those characters who help others to the way of righteousness do so because of their active obedience to Christ's presence. They are motivated by the goodness that this obedience alone generates—not by their particular sectarian alliances or by any self-generated zeal simply to persuade others to adopt their view of religious experience.

THE SAGE

Sage or prophetess figures are to be found in every novel. They offer moral and spiritual instruction that enables the seeker to find himself and embark on the road to spiritual development. These figures tend to be female in the fantasies—recall, for instance, Mara in *Lilith* and the woman in the cottage with four doors in *Phantastes* —but are generally male in the novels. One can only speculate that this is an unconscious result of MacDonald's view of woman and the reality of the fantasy world. Woman stands nearer to the Ideal than man, and the fantasy world stands nearer to the Ideal than does the world of the novel; hence, in the dream world of fantasy women are more suited to giving direction toward the Ideal than men. But in the novels men are often father figures, human surrogates for God the Father, attesting to MacDonald's conviction that fatherhood is at the very heart of the universe. Their approach to the enigmas of life is invariably a carefully reasoned, tightly logical one, unlike the brief, penetrating, authoritative intuitions of women.

MacDonald generally succeeds in drawing these father figures convincingly, but occasionally they are flat and wooden. An example is Mr. Walton, the clergyman whose experiences are detailed in *Annals of a Quiet*

Neighbourhood (1867) and its two sequels, *The Seaboard Parish* (1868) and *The Vicar's Daughter* (1872). These novels are among MacDonald's poorest, lapsing into long sermons illustrated by events that too often challenge one's sense of reality.[4]

Some four years after finishing these chronicles of Mr. Walton's experiences, MacDonald returned to the development of the sage as hero in *Thomas Wingfold, Curate* (1876), and performed his task appreciably better. Wingfold is introduced as a curate who is far from being a paragon of spiritual wisdom and ministry: he is a man of typically professional attitudes who maintains his charge in a leisurely and undistinguished way. At the novel's beginning he is startled when an amiable atheist forces him to admit that he wears the cloth in the Church of England simply as a convenient means of livelihood—that he really neither believes nor disbelieves the doctrines of the church which he purports to serve. Wingfold comes alive to the reader as he responds to this realization; an honest man, he endures intense self-searching and inner turmoil to discover and define his beliefs, all the while continuing to function as clergyman. One is compelled to sympathize with Wingfold, to feel with him the awkwardness of his position, and to follow the logical processes whereby a strong apology for MacDonald's own version of Christian doctrines evolves in Wingfold's mind.

4. The fact that both Greville (*GMDW,* 154) and Bulloch (688) observe that *Annals of a Quiet Neighbourhood* was praised by many readers as being MacDonald's best novel gives an interesting clue to the literary taste and desires of his reading public. More curious yet is the statement of Ronald, whose literary sensibilities appear to be reasonably sharp, that this novel ranks above all his father's other English novels and with the best of the Scottish (*From a Northern Window,* 98).

In finding himself and his faith, Wingfold is helped immeasurably by Joseph Polwarth, a misshapen dwarf who works as a gatekeeper for the large English estate of the parish. Living in humility and poverty with his crippled niece, he perceives the marrow of life in its spiritual aspects, and he quietly helps all who seek him out for his sympathetic counsels. In his wisdom, he is typical of a long list of such figures in the novels, true sages of great moral and spiritual insight who stand outside the conventional Christian ministry. They may be laymen, like Polwarth; schoolmasters, like Mr. Graham in *Malcolm* and *The Marquis Of Lossie*, unconventional and independent ministers, like Mr. Fuller of *Guild Court;* or simply ideal fathers, such as David Elginbrod in *David Elginbrod* and Cosmo Warlock, Sr., in *Warlock O'Glenwarlock*. All are father figures, functioning as surrogates of the heavenly Father to whom they point and whose mercy and compassionate understanding their attitudes exemplify.

Despite this very great dramatic burden resting upon them, many of these characters are remarkably less stereotyped and mechanical than their function. One large difficulty, which ensnares most novelists as they attempt to depict characters of unique goodness, is that a character tends to lose his individuality and hence his interest for the reader in direct proportion to his identification with the Good. Distinct personality traits are invariably diminished, if not lost. But MacDonald believed deeply that God has made each man a unique individual, who can worship God and serve Him in a way no one else can, and that the individual's growth toward spiritual maturity develops, rather than diminishes, this individual uniqueness.[5]

Here is one of many instances, then, in which MacDonald's art is directly shaped by his convictions. Most novelists have less difficulty drawing evil characters than they do good characters; they use evil traits to flesh out and distinguish evil characters, but they tend to see the personalities of the good characters as diluted by goodness. MacDonald has just the opposite difficulty: his good characters are impressively individualistic, whereas his evil characters—such as Beauchamp in *Alec Forbes of Howglen*—are all of a type.[6] This reversal occurred at least partly because MacDonald saw evil as creating a conformity among men that robs them of their distinct individual traits. His success with good characters is also a result of his intensely earnest conviction that he had valid insights into the perennial enigmas of life. The sages in his works understand these enigmas, having themselves grappled successfully with their own personal problems. Therefore, they are able to empathize humbly and compassionately with the heroes in spiritual crises.

For these reasons, MacDonald succeeds in creating in the novels an impressive gallery of characters of great virtue and genuine goodness that are both distinct from each other and convincing in their own right. Their prior interaction with evil and their decisions to resist it have made them free individuals.

5. See "The New Name," *US I*.
6. See Lewis, *Anthology*, 18: "One rare, and all but unique, merit these novels must be allowed. The 'good' characters are always the best and most convincing. His saints live; his villains are stagey."

THE WASTELAND

The decisions of these characters were made during stressful periods in their lives. The wasteland experience of the novels differs from the fantasies in that it represents a period of difficult circumstance which the characters who need spiritual development must face. The wasteland experience is, in the fantasies, an inevitable part of the journey, and, in the novels, the context necessary for spiritual illumination.

These spiritual wastelands take many forms. They may involve a period of sickness, as they do for Juliet Meredith in *Paul Faber, Surgeon,* and Euphra Cameron in *David Elginbrod;* a traumatic discovery, such as when Lady Florimel discovers that she is Malcolm's sister in *The Marquis of Lossie;* or rigorous experiences that transpire "offstage," like the seagoing adventures of Thomas Worboise in *Guild Court.* In *Phantastes,* Anodos falls from the Fairy Palace into a wasteland because of his persistent sensual lusts, and in *Lilith* Vane enters a wasteland as a consequence of disobeying Mr. Raven. The characters in the novels enter their wastelands because they persist in indulging similar vices, generally marked by an undue self-esteem and a general sense of independence from God.

In these wasteland experiences the hero's soul is loosed from all its conventional ties and confidences, his pride is destroyed, and his illusions of self-sufficiency burst. He then discovers himself to be utterly dependent upon the basic spiritual force that sustains life when all its apparent underpinnings are seen to be useless. He is often freed from these attitudes and false securities by events that would normally be considered misfortunes or evil occurrences. In accordance with MacDonald's view of evil, suffering in the novels is often disguised as blessings intended by the heavenly Father to bring the individual to a right orientation to both life and God. These misfortunes penetrate the facades of false selves and enable the individual to discover his true self. As the character comes to acknowledge dependence upon the divine, he is cleansed of past sins and, thus renewed, begins growing toward spiritual maturity.

THE POET

Another archetypal figure that merits attention is that of the poet. He does not appear as unfailingly in MacDonald's works as the other basic images listed above, but he recurs often enough to capture one's attention. These poets provoke a further comparison to the fantasies, particularly *Phantastes*, in which poems have great moral and spiritual power. MacDonald's esteem of the poet is derived from the role that Novalis, the German poet and writer of fantasy, defines in his tale *Heinrich von Ofterdingen:* the poet has great insight into the world of the spirit, and can snatch men away from the familiar present and transport them into that higher region. The world of MacDonald's fantasies is just such a world, and the role of the poet there is to express still deeper insight into the nature of human experience in its ultimate implications.

In the novels, the poet arouses his own spirit and often the spirit of certain sensitive listeners to an awareness of the spiritual world beyond the material world, and he stimulates desire toward it. A good example of the ideal poet in the novels is Donal Grant, the youthful peasant poet in *Sir Gibbie* and *Donal Grant*. He has learned from reading the poetry of Robert Burns something of the poetic power resident in his Scottish language, and Gibbie's spirit feeds upon his rustic ballads while the two tend the cattle on the Scottish hillsides. MacDonald remarks about the function of poetry: "Its true end is to help first the man who makes it along the path to the truth: help for other people may or may not be in it. . . ." Poetry is thus a primary help to the imaginative individual in his pursuit of the truth.

Sir Gibbie is a novel of great charm and one that possesses an impressive quantity of what C. S. Lewis referred to as "holiness." (See the opening remarks from Lewis's *The Great Divorce* in the Introduction.) In its make-up *Sir Gibbie* is more similar to the fantasies than is the average MacDonald novel. The main character, Gibbie, is "one of those few elect natures to whom obedience is a delight—a creature so different from the vulgar that they have but one tentacle they can reach such with—that of contempt." As such he seems suprahuman. Through him MacDonald is imaginatively creating the ideal nature and showing its growth into adulthood.

In his aspirations, his naiveté, and his earnest self-giving for others, Gibbie stands nearer the ideal than is humanly possible, but he is at the same time a delightful creation. MacDonald's power to make goodness interesting is exercised here, and this novel serves as a good introduction to all the novels for the beginning reader.

An invariable trait of MacDonald's potential saints is that they have a poetic sensibility which makes them either poets themselves or lovers of poetry. Donal's songs help Gibbie, who is already "in the kingdom of heaven," though Donal himself has yet to suffer before his entrance. Donal's poems with their spiritual power combine with Janet's reading of Scripture (she is a godly old Scottish woman, one of the few female sages in the novels) to arouse Gibbie's spirit to reach upward after the divine, thus developing his true self.

WOMAN AND THE IDEAL

In addition to receiving help from the sage and the poet, the hero is aided on his spiritual journey by the love of woman. In the last chapter of *Guild Court*, MacDonald muses upon Thomas Worboise's spiritual journey: "The chief aid which Thomas had in this spiritual growth, next to an honest endeavor to do the work of the day and the hour, and his love to Lucy, was the instruction of Mr. Fuller." In this way he ranks these experiences according to their contribution to spiritual growth: next in importance to personal obedience to God, and above that of the spiritual sage, is love of woman. The novels amply illustrate MacDonald's thoughts about how love of woman affects the spirit of man.

The function of young women in the novels also bears close resemblance to that of the marble lady in *Phantastes* and that of Lona in *Lilith*. But in the novels MacDonald does not dwell upon his distinctions between pure attraction and base lust as he did in *Phantastes*. Apparently Victorian taste could cope with that theme presented in fantasy but would not tolerate it in the more realistic world of the novel. The young women in the novels are pure in heart and noble in ideals, and have a large sensitivity for spiritual values. Man's attraction for woman is generally morally pure and acts as a constant inspiration toward the good and a deterrent from the base, giving him incentive to become worthy of her.[7]

In *Paul Faber, Surgeon* (1879), which MacDonald thought was his best novel, he explores quite thoroughly the spiritual effects of love upon both man and woman. The novel offers the possibility that each partner in marriage can function as the other's savior.

Paul Faber is an atheistic doctor, admirable for his honest bearing and humanitarian deeds, living in the same town in which Thomas Wingfold is the curate; in fact, the story is a sequel to the novel about Wingfold. Faber falls in love with one of his patients, Juliet Meredith, a woman who is not a Christian believer but a vague idealist who opposes Faber's rationalism and empiricism. During their courtship MacDonald philosophizes:

> Was he in love with her? . . . The Maker of men alone understands his awful mystery between the man and the woman. But without it, frightful indeed as are

7. MacDonald's view of the effect of the love of woman upon man—which of course, may be traced back to Dante—bears interesting resemblance to that of Tennyson in "Guinevere" of *Idylls of the King:*

> . . . for indeed I knew
> Of no more subtle master under heaven
> Than is the maiden passion for a maid,
> Not only to keep down the base in man,
> But teach high thought, and amiable words
> And courtliness, and the desire of fame,
> And love of truth, and all that makes a man.
>
> (L1. 474–80)

some of its results, assuredly the world he has made would burst its binding rings and fly asunder in shards, leaving his spirit nothing to enter, no time to work his lovely will. . . . Will any man who has ever cast more than a glance into the mysteries of being, dare think himself sufficient to the ruling of his nature? . . . Come thou, holy Love, father of my spirit . . . possess me utterly, for thou art more me than I am myself. Rule thou. . . . And ye, women . . . be the saviours a men, and neither their torment nor their prey!

In the story, Juliet first has the opportunity to be Faber's savior, his guide to truth, not by virtue of any Christian commitment on her part but simply by her role as wife. Like man in general, Faber is not himself capable of ruling his nature without God's help. The experience of love will offer him the possibility of redemption, for it is the immediate expression in his life of God's creative power, ready to be expended to make him the man he is not yet. Juliet's responsibility is awesome, for she must neither torment him by not returning his love, nor allow him simply to use her to satiate his lust; rather, she must be the channel of God's creative power flowing toward him.

But Juliet is not as qualified for this role as she should be. After Faber's ardent courtship overcomes her inexplicable hesitations, she marries him, and then both Faber and the reader discover why she had hesitated: she had been intimate with another man prior to their wedding. This gives Faber the opportunity to be Juliet's savior. Had he himself been the ideal man, he would have fully forgiven her when she confesses to him in utter contrition, and thus would have helped her to become the better person she longs to be. Instead, Faber sees himself as having been duped, sold, married to a slut, and he utterly rejects her, all her love and genuine goodness notwithstanding. In complete dejection, Juliet goes into hiding with the help of a Christian friend; the people of the village think she has drowned herself.[8]

Some time later, as Faber is shown developing a more responsible view of the matter, he muses about his own actions:

> He had deposed her idol—the God who she believed could pardon, and the bare belief in whom certainly could comfort her; he had taken the place with her of that imaginary, yet for some, necessary being; but when, in the agony of repentant shame, she looked to him for the pardon he alone could give her, he had turned from her with loathing, contempt, and insult! He was the one in the whole earth, who, by saying to her Let it be forgotten, could have lifted her into life and hope!

Faber's rejection of her marks him as a man of low moral and spiritual character. The man with a more godlike character would have acted in a manner worthy of God's child by extending to her the forgiveness she sought, thereby exemplifying God's willingness to forgive her. MacDonald uses the biblical incident of the adulterous woman forgiven by Christ with "Neither do I condemn

8. The scene in which Juliet pleads with Paul to whip her for her past indiscretion leads Woolf to conclude MacDonald is exhibiting sadism (*GK*, 306–14). He is well answered by Reis: "If the fictional representation of cruelty and violence is to be taken as symptomatic of their presence in the psychic makeup of every author in whose works they appear, what artist is immune to the accusation? For that matter, perhaps none of us is immune, in which case the observation is not worth making" (59, 60).

thee; go, and sin no more" as a frequent reference throughout this section of the novel.[9]

The full hypocrisy of Faber's action, however, is now revealed to the reader: he discovers in town his own illegitimate daughter. Encountering the child is the first incident that brings Faber to a true realization of the duplicity of his position, and from that time on he begins to move toward moral and spiritual enlightenment. In hiding, Juliet bears their own chid, and in a scene that is strained by coincidence, Faber is called to minister to her in a room kept dark so that he does not recognize her.

But the discovery is made at the opportune time, and the couple is reconciled. In their child there is further expression of the divine mystery of life that is ready to bring them to a fuller knowledge of their true nature before God: "He and she met in that child's life—her being was the eternal fact of their unity. . . . Both she and he had to learn that there was yet a closer bond between them, necessary indeed to the fact that a child *could* be born of them, namely that they two had issued from the one perfect Heart of love." Their child, the fruit of their love, should become a powerful symbol to them of the Love that is at the very core of the universe, and that loves all people into being. Thus, although each previously had failed to guide the other to truth, the experience of having a child offers them another opportunity to discover life's true grace. All of life is sacramental.

CONCLUSION

Perhaps the single strongest impression one takes away from the novels is that of the depth and scope of

9. John 8:11.

MacDonald's sacramentalism. All natural phenomena and all experiences in life are associated with the divine love and have a constant potential to be means of grace. The experiences which befall man because he too is a natural being—birth, procreation, death—are sacred, and should be sources of joy, simply because God is expressing Himself and His nature in them. If man does not respond properly to these experiences, it is because he is not reading God's intentions correctly and is not being obedient to the divine will. At a time when such novelists as Samuel Butler and Thomas Hardy were opposing the idea of revealed religious truth, and were thinking darkly on humanity's lot in a capricious and malignant universe, MacDonald was depicting people as capable of benefiting greatly from inherent truth.

In MacDonald's world people are often guilty of ignoring God's presence and true intentions. Not recognizing God in His works, they exploit life's experiences for the pleasure and profit of the self. They must be saved from various "false selves." Either these fill people with a sense of pride and imagined self-sufficiency, or they (e.g., the rational self) contrive false explanations for the phenomena of life, based upon mere sensual experience or appearances. Those who awaken to the true nature of things nurture the growth of their true selves, a process invariably accompanied by coming into harmony with nature.

For stirring examples of directly receiving God's grace through communion with nature, one need only turn to the scenes in *The Marquis of Lossie* in which Malcolm walks by the seashore or through the woods in the moonlight, or those in *Robert Falconer* in which Robert travels through the continent, or those in *Wilfrid*

Cumbermede in which Wilfrid is lost in awe among the ice caves of the Swiss Alps. The divine essence of man's being is aroused and nourished as quickly by this communion as by any other means. MacDonald is capable of describing the Romantic view of art as developed by Wordsworth: a harmony that exists between a spiritually responsive character and the natural handiwork of his God.[10]

The novels present a vision of life and its meaning which, in its basic analysis, is very much like that of the fantasies. Beneath the complexities of experience MacDonald saw the presence of certain basic patterns, patterns which not only lend structure to his writings but also express the nature of God and His divine grace.

---

10. Referring to depictions of natural disasters, Reis writes: "In these scenes, the habitual diffuseness of MacDonald's style gives way to a precision of description, a vigor of expression, as effective as that of any of the masters of English narrative—among whom MacDonald is not ordinarily to be counted" (60).

Chapter 7

Shadows, Shadows, Shadows All!

"Everyone, however, who feels the story, will read its
meaning after his own nature and development: one
man will read one meaning in it, another will read
another."

–Preface to the 1893 American edition of
The Light Princess and Other Fairy Tales

IN THE FAIRY STORY "The Golden Key," at the
moment when Tangle comes into the presence of the Old
Man of the Fire:

She had a marvellous sense that she was in the secret
of the earth and all its ways. Everything she had seen,
or learned from books; all that her grandmother had
said or sung to her; all the talk of the beasts, birds, and
fishes; all that had happened to her on her journey
with Mossy, and since then in the heart of the earth
with the Old man and the Older man—all was plain:

she understood it all, and saw that everything meant
the same thing, though she could not have put it into
words again.

Students of mythology tell us that the effects a religious
man feels in the presence of his myths are similar to those
described in this passage. Tangle is on her way to the land
"from whence the shadows fell"—the land of ultimate
reality. The world of myth transcends profane time and
space; it is the real world of being, where ultimate meaning resides and from which it comes. Tangle has arrived
at a place and moment in which "all was plain"—all her
past experiences have become meaningful to her. This
meaning has an astonishing unity to it: it shines through
the complexities of life, reconciling contradictory
elements and revealing an essential, ineffable simplicity,
a conformity of import and purpose.

Among literary genres, only mythopoeia can capture
and present such a vision. While "The Golden Key" is
perhaps MacDonald's finest effort in this genre, in
general the mythic element in the fairy stories is somewhat more subdued. The reason may be that he has the
sheer entertainment of children in mind. Because the
tales contain more of the absurd and the tone is more
light and playful, fresh breakthroughs into the transcendent are more rare.

An additional reason for briefly discussing the fairy
tales is that their themes have been presented more
compellingly to the adult mind in the longer fantasies;
the fairy tales dilute and simplify these themes so that
children can understand them. This can be illustrated by
juxtaposing the fairy story "The Giant's Heart" and the

episode of the wooden men who oppose the little girl trying to grow wings in chapter 23 of *Phantastes*. The theme in both stories is similar: true children of God can receive serious spiritual harm from "good churchmen" whose humanity has been seriously distorted because of the religious attitudes they have acquired from the institutionalized church. The counterpart of the wooden men in this fairy tale is the giant who has given his heart to an eagle to care for in her far-off nest. " 'It's a fretting care to have a heart of one's own to look after,' " he complains to his wife. " 'The responsibility is too much for me.' " As an evidence of his debased moral and spiritual state, he crassly fattens little children and eats them like radishes.

The little girl and boy featured in the tale, Tricksey-Wee and Buffy-Bob, wander into Giantland and find their own lives threatened by the giant. They try to set things right by learning from the birds of the wood where the giant's heart is being kept. Then they make the perilous journey to the eagle's nest atop Mount Skycrack, helped by a horde of obliging spiders. Having retrieved the heart, they return it to the giant only after he promises to be better. But the giant reneges on his promise, and the tale ends with little Buffy-Bob felling him with his trusty pocketknife.

The moral is clear: one should keep his heart, and not trust another with its nurture. To be lazy, as the giant is, and place it in another's care is morally reprehensible, and results in destroying one's own humanity. One notes with interest that Mount Skycrack is described as looming in the distance "like the spire of a church. . . ." The parallel suggested between the mountain and the

institutionalized church is strengthened as one recalls
MacDonald's general attitude toward the church, and his
unhappiness with its shortcomings. To abandon one's
heart to its care is a prescription for spiritual retrogression. Thus the tale makes a point very similar to that
made by the incident of the wooden men in *Phantastes*,
yet here the focus is more upon the story and its
entertainment value. One does not feel the imaginative
strength of statement that made the longer adult fantasy
so powerful.

The tale of the giant's heart is one of many fairy tales
which first appeared in the somewhat curious novel *Adela
Cathcart*. In this novel MacDonald offers an interesting
theory of the moral nature and purpose of the fairy tale—
and of all imaginative literature that springs from a truly
Christian imagination. The work contains within a
framework of realistic narrative a number of experiments
in symbolic tales, from fairy story to various moral
anecdotes to parable. The plot cleverly allows their
telling. A group of relatives and friends gather in Colonel
Cathcart's country home during the Christmas holidays,
but their merriment is curtailed by his daughter Adela's
strange illness, for which no medical remedy has been
found. A new doctor is summoned, a young man of
unorthodox medical notions, who feels that her ailment
is spiritual rather than physical. He proposes a remedy of
storytelling, whereby the group meets on appointed
evenings and listens to the contribution of one of its
various members.

The cure is wondrously successful. Adela not only is
cured, but in the end marries the doctor. MacDonald
speculates in the novel that all disease ultimately has a

moral source, inasmuch as man belongs to a fallen race; hence, individuals who are ill may often profit more from moral and spiritual ministrations than from physical ones. The imagination is indispensable to this kind of aid, because it can present a vision of truth necessary for spiritual well-being.

Two other of MacDonald's stories that are often included in collections of his fairy tales appear in *Adela Cathcart*. Seeing them in the context of that novel proves helpful in understanding them. One is "The Light Princess," which is the first story to be told to the ailing Adela, a model demonstration of MacDonald's theory of the salutary effect of a good tale. The story is one of the "lightest" MacDonald ever wrote, filled with punning, and characterized by a generally pixieish tone. The theme is similar to that of the story of Cosmo in *Phantastes:* true love is self-giving; one must die to live.

SACRAMENTALISM IN THE FAIRY TALES

The other of the more familiar fairy tales that first appeared in *Adela Cathcart* is "The Shadows." The theme is in harmony with MacDonald's sacramental view of nature and circumstances, considering as it does the good moral effect that shadows have upon people's consciences. The story concerns a sick old man who in delirium has a vision of fairies taking him to the Land of Shadows. There he learns of the many ways in which shadows have helped men achieve moral and spiritual growth in this world. They frighten people during moments of wrongdoing, thus lessening the amount of evil in the world.

The evil effects of a purely rationalist approach to life are aptly exposed in "The Day Boy and the Night Girl" (otherwise titled "The History of Photogen and Nycteris"), a story that is remarkably relevant for our increasingly rationalistic, information-gathering age. It relates the evil actions of Watho, a witch "who desired to know everything. . . . She cared for nothing in itself— only for knowing it." This penchant is depicted as a wolf in her mind. She raises two children in two different ways: a boy, Photogen, so that he is aware only of day, thinking it the only reality; and a girl, Nycteris, so that she is aware only of the night, in turn thinking it the only reality. How Photogen discovers the night and Nycteris the day, and their correspondingly fresh and wonderful new ways of seeing the world, occupies most of the story. When Nycteris escapes into the night, leaving the per-petual darkness of the cave in Watho's castle where she was raised, she is rapturously delighted with the wonders of nature under the moon. On the other hand, Photogen, familiar only with daylight, is very frightened when he first discovers darkness. But the two meet one night, and Nycteris helps Photogen orient himself to the night as he helps her know the delights of the day. One day after Photogen kills a werewolf that attacks them, they discover it is Watho he has slain, and they subsequently inherit her castle. The story ends with their anticipating a still greater day to come as so many of the fairy stories do, engendering a sense of progress toward a higher experience of life.

The story underscores MacDonald's eclectic spirit towards inadequate views of reality, systems in conflict because their concerns are confined only to what fits neatly into pat mental structures. These are products of pure rationalism, the bent of the human spirit that cares only to be right in its knowing. Such differences may disappear in the presence of larger views of reality—those that take into account the aspect of human nature that must feed on myth. Rationalist frictions are reduced in importance, and people may find underneath them a basis for mutual understanding. Life grasped in its depth is sacramental.

TRIUMPH OVER EVIL

MacDonald's sacramentalism is also a significant element in his fairy story, "Little Daylight," which appears in the middle of the previously discussed *At the Back of the North Wind.* This story develops the theme that evil ultimately results in good: the heroine finally breaks free of an evil fairy's curse, finding herself a stronger and better person because of it.

Indeed, MacDonald's fairies seem to be more often evil than good, with their machinations being foiled in an entertaining manner. He is generally careful to integrate whatever moral intentions he has in a particular story with its aesthetic structure, so that the effect is seldom preachy. A good example is the tale "The Carasoyn," which works obliquely with the theme of becoming.

The rather complex plot concerns a shepherd boy, Colin, and the difficulties he encounters because of a horde of fairies. Twice he falls prey to their chicaneries, once as a boy and later as a grown man. In order to extricate himself from each predicament, he must perform a task outlined for him by an old woman, a figure not unlike the great-grandmother of the Curdie stories. She can only be found when the seeker loses himself—a variation of the dying-to-live theme.

Colin undertakes the first task the old woman assigns him in order to free a little girl the fairies are holding prisoner. He must obtain a bottle of a rare Carasoyn wine for the Queen of the Fairies. When he delivers it to the eager queen and she drinks of it, she and her company suddenly become aged and wrinkled. (Carosyn wine is only for really good people, we are told; hence, it ages the evil fairies.) Here is an interesting recurrence of another theme from the Curdie stories. One recalls how the old queen Irene, so glorious in her appearance to Curdie and his father, was Old Mother Wotherwop to the coarse-minded miners. Only people who have grown to be good themselves can recognize and appreciate true goodness. The wicked, who cannot recognize it because it is too far beyond the grasp of their current moral state, may actually be harmed by it. As depicted in Curdie's experience with the fire of roses, good may be immediately terrible.

Colin's second adventure with the fairies occurs when he is a man. Having married the girl whom he previously rescued from the fairies, he loses his child to them in a kidnapping. He performs a similar task at the instruction of the same old woman, finds the fairies, and rescues his son—but this time Colin extracts a sworn promise from them not to annoy his family again. And thus the story closes: the evil fairies have been foiled, their activities having accomplished no permanent harm, and those characters who have been extricated from their power are better beings because of their encounters.

Colin triumphs because of his courage and his determination to help those in distress. Another story that gives an intriguing presentation of this theme is "Cross Purposes," a story that is more symmetrical than most of MacDonald's tales. The narrative opens with the Queen of Fairyland commissioning a fairy and a goblin, Peasebottom and Toadstool, to bring two mortals to her domain for her entertainment. Peasebottom entices a girl named Alice to make the trip; she is a spoiled little girl who is bored with her life and desires to leave home to follow the sunset. Toadstool brings Richard, a Curdie-like little boy whose poverty has molded him into a solid and promising character. Alice and Richard meet en route to Fairyland, and both have second thoughts about their journey. Since fairies are rendered powerless against mortals as soon as the mortals exercise their wills against the fairies' schemes, Peasebottom and Toadstool disappear, and Alice and Richard are left to find their way back home on their own.

They are lost. As Richard heroically tries to befriend Alice, she rebuffs him, sullen and snobbish. In their ensuing adventures, however, she finds that to withdraw from Richard envelops her in a frightening loneliness, so that she comes to feel that "there was no one in the universe but herself." Coming to her wits' end, she runs to Richard for help. This incident, swiftly drawn, depicts that turning point in the moral experience of people that MacDonald speaks of on numerous occasions, both in his sermons and in his novels. It is, he hopes, the experience that all men who are growing morally worse, retrogress-ing on the scale of becoming, will have sooner or later, in this world or another. The definitive depiction of this idea occurs in *Lilith*, in the scene in which Vane meets the skeletons in the nether world: the loneliness and silence of darkness, in which the hellish fantasies of the depraved individuals' tormented souls have free reign, are the ultimate goad to his turning. In the fairy tale Alice has but the slightest taste of all this.

Richard has fallen in love with Alice. In the darkness he is excited when he thinks that her face gives off light by which he can see the path. But MacDonald explains what is actually happening: "The fact was, that the moment he began to love Alice, his eyes began to send forth light. What he thought came from Alice's face, really came from his eyes. All about her and her path he could see, and every minute saw better; but to his own path he was blind." This occurrence intriguingly suggests the nature and power of love: love enables a person to see another sympathetically. The result is that Alice begins to have a similar experience, thinking that Richard's face lights the path, and because each sees the other's path clearly, they get on well. Real love is requited, and a way opens in the darkness.

Finding home, however, is not easy. In a passage in which MacDonald uses the "anything-can-happen" quality of dreams to give us a convincing experience of the unexpected that may continually occur in Fairyland, Richard and Alice face several baffling difficulties. The two overcome each one by an act of defiant courage. They finally see each other as far apart—on opposite sides of a great chasm, many feet across, with the gap between them many feet deep. In their distress Richard decides this too is a trick, and when both jump courageously toward the other, they discover what appeared to be a great expanse is only a gap a foot or two wide and deep. As a reward for their courage the Queen of Fairyland grants them free and unmolested passage to her realm whenever they please.

The process of spiritual becoming, which is depicted in Alice's experience, has a more thorough presentation in the longer fairy story "The Wise Woman." The plot focuses upon two girls: Rosamond, a princess, and Agnes, a shepherd's daughter. Both are seriously spoiled by their parents, so that each becomes very conceited. This moral ugliness brings each in turn to the Wise Woman who lives in the wood, a figure not unlike Queen Irene in the Curdie stories. Through various experiences with her, both girls learn self-discipline and humility. Much of the charm of the story lies in its consistent blend of playfulness and seriousness, together with its strongly realistic depiction of the slow, agonizing process whereby moral lessons are learned and virtue is acquired. The transformations are not facile: they are as preciously achieved as those of real life. Though MacDonald's narrator in "The Wise Woman" insists that the fairyland of the story is a very different type of world from our own, the reader concludes that the import of experiences in both worlds is very much the same.

LONGING FOR FAIRYLAND

Consistently in MacDonald's fantasies, to achieve admittance to Fairyland is a prize that answers a deep longing in people's hearts. Fairyland, a realm in the imagination, is a type of intermediate world between the one we know and that of humanity's ultimate destination. It is a higher world, one of glory and wonder. People of different spiritual sensitivities and needs arrive by different routes, and often became fit for the atmosphere by receiving there a fuller portion of life. These ideas are presented with great appeal in "The Golden Key," the finest of the fairy tales.

The boy and girl in this story are named Mossy and Tangle. Mossy finds a golden key at the foot of a glorious rainbow, and sets out in quest of the lock which it will open. He is joined in his quest by Tangle, a little girl from the same village. They meet in the cottage of a wise old woman, who cleanses, refreshes, and directs them on their way.

MacDonald's belief in the upward mobility of life, with all living things becoming freer and more beautiful as they grow in spiritual wisdom, is set forth in the incident of the fishlike creatures of the lady's cottage. They act as messengers, bringing the children to her cottage and generally doing her bidding, while waiting expectantly for the day when they will be eaten by the people of Fairyland. That is their ambition, for it is "their highest end in that condition." But this consummation is not their final end: they arise phoenixlike from the fire upon which they have been prepared—creatures with a more glorious incarnation—and are released to a larger freedom.

Leaving the old lady's cottage, Mossy and Tangle travel through a strange valley filled only with intriguing shadows, and they long to find "the country whence the shadows fell." The valley vaguely suggests this present world seen from a Platonic point of view: its substances are only shadows. The children's journey through it makes them age, Mossy's hair becoming streaked with grey, and Tangle developing wrinkles in her forehead. As they reach the borders of the valley, Tangle loses Mossy in a poignant scene that suggests all the pathos of that moment when aged persons lose their life's mate. Each then goes on his way alone, separately meeting, after various difficulties, the Old Man of the Sea. Tangle meets him first, and then goes on to meet two other figures, the Old Man of the Earth and the still older Old Man of the Fire. The latter is able to direct her to "the country whence the shadows fell," where all the characters of the story long to go.

Tangle's meeting with the Old Man of the Fire is one of the most fascinating passages in the entirety of MacDonald's writings. To Tangle's wonder, she finds him to be like "a marvellous Child" engaged in a mysterious game "of infinite meaning." MacDonald is at his best in a descriptive passage that must speak for itself:

> There was such an awfulness of absolute repose on the face of the child that Tangle stood dumb before him. He had no smile, but the love in his large grey eyes was deep as the centre. And with the repose there lay on his face a shimmer as of moonlight, which seemed as if any moment it might break into such a ravishing smile as would cause the beholder to weep himself to death. But the smile never came, and the moonlight lay there unbroken. For the heart of the child was too deep for any smile to reach from it to his face.

A reader who knows MacDonald's sermons is reminded
of the one entitled "A Child in the Midst,"[1] in which
MacDonald argues that of all the comparisons one can
make between God and man, God is most like the
essence of ideal childhood. God is no "great King on a
grand throne, thinking how grand he is, and making it
the business of his being and the end of his universe to
keep up his glory." Rather, ". . . he alone can be perfectly,
abandonedly simple and devoted. . . . It is his childlikeness that makes him our God and Father." The sermon
gives the concept compelling exposition; the powerful
myth of the fairy tale presents to our imaginations the
beauty of the truth itself. Each of the old men in the
myth are separate perceptions of God who appropriately
accommodates himself in grace to all to whom he
appears, matching their perceptions with their human
needs.

Tangle's route differs from the one Mossy takes.
With the golden key in hand, he proceeds by a different
way to meet the Old Man of the Sea. Because Mossy's
feet are very weary, he receives a bath in the Old Man's
inner cave and is wondrously refreshed. The Old Man
explains:

> "You have tasted of death now....Is it good?"
> "It is good," said Mossy. "It is better than life."
> "No," said the Old Man: "it is only more life.
> Your feet will make no holes in the water now."

Thus enabled to continue his journey atop the waves of
the sea, he comes to a great precipice of rock, and
climbing halfway up, he is momentarily stopped by an

1. *US I.*

impassable cliff, until he sees in the face of the rock a small keyhole surrounded with sapphires. The key fits, the rock barrier falls away, and Mossy climbs a rainbow stair into Tangle's presence. They happily discover that they both are now beings of great beauty and nobility, "younger and better, stronger and wiser, than they had ever been before." Together they joyously climb the rainbow with its riotous splendor of color, moving toward the "country whence the shadows fall."

The careful reader is always wary of taking a symbolic tale too far in the direction of allegory, hunting for precise meanings when meaning is suggested only in the general pattern and occasional elements of the story. One cannot help but be intrigued, however, by the different routes Mossy and Tangle must take between their parting and their reunion at the foot of the rainbow. It is Mossy who has the golden key, which seems to be a symbol of the imagination in its capacity to envision and desire eternity. Mossy's imagination was nurtured and exercised in his youth in a manner MacDonald advocates in his novels and essays when he theorizes about how children are to be educated imaginatively. As a child, Mossy learned of the existence of the golden key from his great-aunt while listening to her stories. He earned his name by his habit of sitting all day long upon a moss-covered stone, reading stories. In the process, his innate desire for a higher and better world grew strong.

It may be helpful to recall Wordsworth's famous lines from *The Prelude* in a passage from book 6, in which he describes the function of the imagination as establishing within man the certainty of his immortality:

> Our destiny, our being's heart and home,
> Is with infinitude, and only there;
> With hope it is, hope that can never die,
> Effort, and expectation, and desire,
> And something evermore about to be.

It is the imagination that enables man to see beyond the immediate to the eternal, establishing the conviction that his destiny is "only there." To cultivate this aspect of his being is to further the realization of his desire. Mossy's key, respected by all the characters he meets, shortens his journey through the nether world and gains him easy access to his destination.

Tangle, on the other hand, who has no key, must travel a longer, more tedious route to the same destination. As a child she was less fortunate than Mossy: she was "neglected and left untidy." Frightened into Fairyland by mischievous fairies (who inadvertently do her great good), she has a longer interview in the Wise Woman's cottage than does Mossy, and her general progress through the nether world is slower. After meeting the Old Man of the Sea she must visit the Old Man of the Earth, and then the Old Man of the Fire. On her way to the latter she passes through a scorching fire that seems more than she can bear; after her meeting with the Old Man of the Fire, a serpent leads her to her destination. One is inclined to see in these events indications that Tangle's route—that of the unimaginative and less fortunate individual— is one by which wisdom is gained from more direct experiences with evil, and holiness is acquired from a more direct purging.

Comparisons may be drawn between this story and the closing chapters of *Lilith*, in which the party of characters there make "the journey home" to the Father of the Universe. MacDonald's achievement in creating an aura that answers longings deep within the heart, an aura that suggests abounding joy and an ever-increasing good upon the upward journey of life, scarcely has its peer in this type of literature. "The Golden Key" is a masterpiece in literary myth.

Chapter 8

Showing the
Unshowable

"Law is the soil in which alone beauty will grow;
beauty is the only stuff in which Truth can be clothed;
and you may, if you will, call Imagination the tailor
that cuts her garments to fit her. . . ."

—Preface to the 1893 American edition of
The Light Princess and Other Fairy Tales

TODAY, MANY WHO THINK about the relation of
Christianity to art discern an incompatibility between
them. They see art, by its very nature, as having to be free
and unconstrained by dogma, and Christianity as arbi-
trary and confining. Such people would be quick to see
MacDonald as a man torn between two worlds. Having
failed as a minister in the established church, he turned
to his second love, imaginative writing, and attempted to
reconcile it to his purpose, using it as a substitute for the

pulpit. His true artistic talent, struggling for breath under a great blanket of dogma, is all but stifled.

But it must be observed that any man's art bears deepest relation to his view of the meaning of life, whether he intends it that way or not. No artist's work can exist apart from his faith, whether his belief be Christian or otherwise. In MacDonald's system of belief, nothing is more compatible, nothing is more unified in nature, intent, and purpose, than art and faith.

As he states in the above epigraph, "Beauty is the only stuff in which Truth can be clothed," and the imagination cuts the clothes. Any deficiencies in MacDonald's art may be attributed to a weakness in his imagination—not to his faith.

CHIEF INFLUENCES

Three chief influences shaped MacDonald's view of the nature and function of the imagination: German Romanticism, Coleridge, and certain Christian mystics such as Swedenborg. Evidently MacDonald discovered the German Romantics during his college days. He was already at that time skeptical of the capacity of Calvinism—or of any strict, logical system of abstractions—to contain truth. The Germans—E. T. A. Hoffmann and Friedrich von Hardenberg (Novalis) were his favorites—taught that truth was first received by the imagination and the intuition, and then rationally apprehended. This apparently confirmed what he already felt to be true. After all, did not the ancient Hebrew prophets, such as Ezekiel, present the reader with visions to be interpreted rather than with systems of thought to be learned by rote? Did not biblical writers in general present depictions of human experience in narrative form rather than arguments derived from abstract systems of thought?

Coleridge was another strong influence on MacDonald. Stephen Prickett points out how closely MacDonald's theory and practice derive from that of Coleridge, and what type of additions MacDonald makes. The central framework for Coleridge's thought is that of the existence of two worlds: the "I am" and the "It is," the subjective and the objective. Symbols bring these two worlds together in reciprocal relationship, and the poet's imagination is a symbolizing faculty. Coleridge celebrated the character of Scripture because of the manner in which these two realms of meaning seemed to him to coincide in its narratives: "In the Scriptures therefore both facts and persons must of necessity have a two-fold significance, a past and a future, a temporary and a perpetual, a particular and a universal application. They must be at once Portraits and Ideals."[1] In much of his poetry, such as *The Ancient Mariner*, he sought to incorporate these two realms.

Similarly, MacDonald's fictional writings integrate and intermingle two worlds, the immediate physical world and the spiritual realm immanent within it. The imagined realm of Faerie, through a system of symbolic correspondences, presents these as interdependent and interrelated. As we have noted elsewhere, the mysticism in MacDonald's theory of correspondences is influenced by his readings in Böhme, Blake, and Law. His union of mysticism with Scottish Calvinist severity, impacted by

1. *The Statesman's Manual*, as quoted in Prickett, 18.

Coleridge's thought and the eclectic spirit of German Romanticism, enabled MacDonald to achieve his synthesized vision.

VIEW OF THE IMAGINATION

Convinced the imagination is essential to apprehending spiritual truth, MacDonald boldly developed a comprehensive theory of its nature and working. In his essay, "The Imagination: Its Functions and Its Culture," printed in *Orts*, MacDonald writes: ". . . we dare to claim for the true, childlike humble imagination, such an inward oneness with the laws of the universe that it possesses itself an insight into the very nature of things." He continues to argue that the imagination must be colaborer with the intellect; otherwise thinking is merely analytic and sterile.

In this colaboring, MacDonald concludes, the primary function of the imagination is to give forms to thought. These forms are not original with people, however; they come from nature, which God has made. In fact, God is constantly in the process of creating both nature and people: everything is presently being thought by God. Hence, to think imaginatively is to think God's thoughts after Him.

Further, since God continues to think the forms of nature, He is constantly investing them with meaning. All of them mean humanity well—they are sacramental. People, thinking imaginatively, will come to know some of these meanings when they are morally and spiritually in harmony with God. The quotation above stipulates that the imagination must be "true, childlike," and "humble." What MacDonald means by these qualities, and how essential he feels them to be, have been discussed throughout this book.

MacDonald's view of the extent to which insightful thinking depends upon God is perhaps made more clear by a poem he wrote, entitled "A Cry":

Lord, hear my discontent: all blank I stand,
A mirror polished by thy hand;
Thy sun's beams flash and flame from me—
I cannot help it: here I stand, there he!
To one of them I cannot say,
Go, and on yonder water play;
Nor one poor ragged daisy can I fashion—
I do not make the words of this my limping passion!
If I should say, Now I will think a thought,
Lo, I must wait, unknowing
What thought in me is growing,
Until the thing to birth be brought!
Nor know I then what next will come
From out the gulf of silence dumb:
I am the door the thing will find
To pass into the general mind!
I cannot say I think—
I only stand upon the thought-well's brink:
From darkness to the sun the water bubbles up—
I lift it in my cup.
Thou only thinkest—I am thought;
Me and my thought thou thinkest. Naught
Am I but as a fountain spout
From which thy water welleth out.
Thou art the only one, the all in all.—
Yet when my soul on thee doth call
And thou dost answer out of everywhere,
I in thy allness have my perfect share.

God is all in all. The true person delights in this truth; the false person cringes in its presence, striving to maintain a sense of autonomy, as Lilith does when she encounters Mara. This poem is a prayer spoken by a voice intimate with God and completely submissive to Him, waiting to be invested with true thoughts. The precise thoughts God can give anyone are those appropriate to one's spiritual state at the time. MacDonald's views may seem to some to be completely fatalistic, but what keeps them from being so in his mind is the freedom of the will to obey God's precepts and to grow into a higher state of being, or conversely, to revel in supposed autonomy, sinking still further in the scale of being toward "the animals' country," as previously noted. People determine the quality of their thoughts indirectly, through their decisions as to whether or not to obey God's precepts.

God is entirely benevolent and trustworthy, ever working for people's spiritual growth. But He honors free decisions, and one's will does control the *quality* of thoughts one receives. If an individual wills to keep his mind and imagination clean, God may be trusted to give an appreciable amount of truth. MacDonald's insistence upon the freedom of the will, with the blend he achieves between the two imponderables of divine sovereignty and human responsibility, is not unlike Augustine's.

MacDonald also believed that the thoughts God gives the artist, expressed in their appropriate beauty in art, have an especial power to arouse virtuous feelings in his readers. This, too, is an idea derived from Novalis, who in his tale *Heinrich von Ofterdingen* teaches that the true spirit of fable and virtue are the same, and the former ministers to the latter. A good illustration of this principle can be found in *Phantastes*. When Anodos, in obedience to the woman of the cottage with the four doors, leaves to perform a noble deed, he is commissioned to help the two brothers rid their father's land of the three giants who are despoiling it. Anodos's mandate is to sing his songs to them, which arouse the brothers to virtuous and valorous actions. Clearly, the songs, or the art they represent, have the power to inspire good deeds. One recalls as well the power of song in the Curdie stories. MacDonald's belief in this power must have been a strong factor in enabling him to leave the pastorate and devote his life to literary creation.

INCOHERENCE AND UNDERLYING MEANING

In the two worlds of people's experience—the inner world of consciousness and the outer world of nature—MacDonald perceived both a surface incoherence and an underlying meaning. In his imaginative prose writings he undertook to incorporate each of these, and to penetrate the incoherence with the meanings he saw, an undertaking that he felt required a certain spiritual maturity. Again, he found his authority in Novalis.

Phantastes is prefaced with a three-paragraph epigraph taken from Novalis's theories on the nature of the fairy tale, or märchen (translated from the German), which presents the following principles. A fairy tale is like a dream-picture without coherence, a story controlled by association that has only a general allegorical meaning. But in the tale all of nature must express the entire world of the spirit. The world of the fairy tale must be entirely different from, and yet at the same time bear a similarity to, the true world, as chaos is similar to creation. It must also have a musical harmony. This, in summary, appears to be the basic literary theory that shaped *Phantastes* and all of MacDonald's succeeding fantasies, and what accounts for their primary characteristics: the surface incoherence, the dreamlike quality, the generalized symbolical intention, the relationships between the world of nature and the world of spirit and the musical orchestration of themes.[2]

This combination of a surface incoherence with an underlying harmony characterizes both the outer world and the realm of the mind mirrored in the visions of the imagination created by art. The meanings and purposes of God infuse the entirety of this apparent chaos with a "harmony within." The spiritually mature artist is able to catch glimpses of the true import of things. The glory of God's purposes is such that, when at last they are more fully revealed to those capable of receiving the revelation, the recipients will be satisfied in awe.

MacDonald never claims for himself the spiritual maturity that is, in his system of thought, the sine qua non for complete understanding. To him, pontificating would be certain evidence that the inferior self—the death of which is the prime essential to spiritual health— is very much alive and well; hence, anyone with such an attitude would be patently deluding himself.

2. Manlove quotes selected lines from "A Cry" and, after considering certain aspects of MacDonald's theory, complains of his trying to "have it both ways," of being "simultaneously 'chaotic' and responsible" (66). He then proceeds to find fault with both levels of MacDonald's art. He appears unwilling to allow MacDonald his view concerning the role that God plays in man's being and in his world. MacDonald assumes the complete trustworthiness of God.

CONCLUSION

Such, then, is the general blend of literary and theological convictions that shaped George MacDonald's fictional worlds. MacDonald wants the incidents to both baffle his readers and make a certain sense to them, as events in the actual world of human experience did to him. One would expect that any author undertaking this sort of task would at times produce material that is unduly private in character and import—and MacDonald's work is sometimes just that. In addition, a disturbing amount of his work, though it has virtue in abundance, lacks an aesthetically pleasing art form; MacDonald wrote too quickly and too prolifically to be as careful a stylist as he should have been. Nevertheless, MacDonald's best attempts in literary myth, of which "The Golden Key" is an example, have genuine power. This power comes partly from the conviction he succeeds in arousing within his readers that he is exploring spiritual experience in an imaginatively significant manner.

Successful myths rise to probe the ultimate mysteries of existence, simultaneously arousing the reader's wonder and awakening in him a desire that these insights be true. The reader becomes convinced that they bring him into closer proximity to the Ultimate Mystery, which stands considerably beyond the reach of any system of abstract principles. One feels as though one is receiving intimations of a life beyond this. In his better fantasies MacDonald's writing has this effect. He felt that creating literary myths was the most effective method of imaginatively exploring and communicating his deeply held religious convictions. In so doing, he projected imagined worlds that have a "harmony within," that answer some of man's deepest curiosities and desires, and, through the power of myth, show the unshowable. It is in this mythopoeic art that he excels, an achievement that makes him deserving of a prominent place in any listing of literary mythmakers.

Appendix:

A Year With
George MacDonald

Each day read one stanza from *A Book of Strife in the Form of a Diary of an Old Soul.* (Johannesen publishes this with Rampolli.)

Each month read one novel, one fantasy, and one sermon. Use the "Glossary of Scottish Terms" with the Scottish novels, and read all of them in the unabridged, unedited editions.

January: *Sir Gibbie,* "The Golden Key,"
    and "The Child in the Midst" (*US I*).
February: *Donal Grant, The Princess and the Goblin,*
    and "The Creation in Christ" (*US III*).
March: *Thomas Wingfold,* "The Light Princess,"
    and "The Knowing of the Son" (*US III*).
April: *Paul Faber,* "The Day Boy and the Night Girl,"
    and "Life" (*US II*).
May: *Weighed and Wanting, Phantastes,*
    and "The Consuming Fire" (*US I*)
June: *David Elginbrod,* "The Giant's Heart,"
    and "Life" (*US II*).
July: *Robert Falconer, Lilith,*
    and "The Voice of Job" (*US II*).
August: *Wilfrid Cumbermede,* "The Wise Woman,"

and "Self-Denial" (*US II*).
September: *Malcolm, At the Back of the North Wind,*
   and "The God of the Living" (*US I*).
October: *Alec Forbes of Howglen,* "The Shadows,"
   and "The Last Farthing" (*US II*).
November: *What's Mine's Mine, The Princess and Curdie,*
   and "Justice" (*US III*).
December: *There and Back,* "Cross Purposes,"
   and "Freedom" (*US III*).

Glossary of
Scottish Terms

a'but: about
ae: one
again': against
ahin': behind
Aiden: Eden (Gaelic)
ain: own
airt: region
aith: oath
amaist: almost
ance: once
ane: one
aneath: beneath
arles: earnest
a'thegither: altogether
athort: across
aucht: eight
auld: old
ava: at all
aye: certainly, surely
ayont: beyond
ayr: heir (Gaelic)
bairn: child
baith: both
ballant: a fish
bane: bone

barkit: covered
bauchles: boots
bawbee: a halfpenny
bed: remained
beir: to bear
bejan: first year
          undergraduate
benn: behind
bick: bitch
bide: wait
bien: comfortable
big: make, build
bigget: built
biggin': building
binna: be not (isn't)
birstled: scorched
bit: spot, place
blastie: gust of wind
blate: bashful
blaud: spoil
blecks: beats, confounds
bluid: blood
boatle: bottle
bools: marbles
bothie: hut, cottage

bourach: heap
bowie: cask
bowster: bolster
brackin': breaking
brae: ascent
braw: good, brave
brig: bridge
broos: eyebrows
brunstane: brimstone
bude: must
buff an' styte: stuff and
    nonsense
buikie: book
bunce: bounce
burnie: brooklet
buss: bush
byganes: bygones
byous: exceedingly
ca: drive
callant: lad
caller: color; cool, fresh
camstairie: perverse
cankert: cross
carden: garden (Gaelic)
carr: calves
Carritchis: catechism
cauf: oaf
caw: search
chap: strike
chappit: struck
chaumer: chamber, room
cheirs: chairs
chimla: chimney
chits: sweetbreads
chop: shop
claes: clothes

claick: clack, harsh call of
    a goose
clash-pyet: tell-tale
clavers: silly gossip
cleuks: claws
clortit: dirty
cluicks: clutches
clype: tell tales
collieshangie: outbreak
compleen: complain
coo: cow
coot: good (Gaelic)
corp: corpse, body
cracks: conversation
crafe: grave (Gaelic)
crap: crept
crater, crayter: creature
creysh: grease
croon: crown
croudin': cooing
cupples: cupolas
curytes: petticoats
darg: day's work
daun'er: stroll
daur: dare
dauty: pet
dawtie: daughter
dee: die
deid: dead
Deil: Devil
denner: dinner
deowty: duty
dingin': becoming dark
dinna: don't
dirl: knock, sound
disjaskit: dilapidated,

exhausted

disna: doesn't

divot: thin piece of sod for
    thatching

dochter: daughter

dockit: deprived

doo: dove

dooms: absolutely

doonhertit: downhearted

doonricht: downright

doot: doubt

douce: quiet, respectable

doun: down

draan: drawn

drap: drop

dune: done

durk: Highland dagger

duv: do

dwyned: dwindled

ear': early

edder: adder

een: eyes

efterhin: afterwards

eident: diligent

eleck: elect

eneuch: enough

Erse: Irish, Gaelic

even: equal

fa'in: falling

fallow: fellow

fan': felt

fand: found

fa's: falls

fash: trouble, annoyance

fashous: troublesome

fause: false

fau't: fault

fecht: fight

fegs: faith

ferlie: wonder

fess: fetch

fin: feel

fit: foot

flannin: flannel

flech: flea

flee: fly

fleg: fright

fleyt: frightened

flykes: trifles

flytit: scolded

forhooit: forsook

fower: unit of currency

fowk: folks, people

frae: from

freits: frets, superstitions

frichtit: frightened

fund'd: founded

fut: foot

gaed: went

gait: way

gang: go on; gone; going

gar, gart: to make, oblige

gey: considerably

ghaist: ghost

ghem: game

gie: give

gien, gin: if

girse: grass

gleds: kites

gleg: quick, keen

gomeril: fool

goon: gown

goukmey: grey gurnard (fish)
gowk: fool
greit: weep
grew: greyhound
grue: feel terror
grummle: grumble
grun': ground
grutten: wept
guddle: mangle
Gude: God
guid: good
haddick: one who is addicted
hae: have
hail: whole
hame: home
han: almost
hantle: a good deal, great
    many
harling: applying a
    composition of sand
    and gravel
hause: throat
haud: hold, restrain
havers: foolish talk
haythen: heathen
heid: head
hemmer: hammer
hert: heart
het: heated
hinner en: extremity,
    termination
hinnie: honey
hirple: limp, walk lamely
hoo: how
hoosie: house
hoot: exclamatory remark

host: cough
houp: hope
howdie: midwife
howkin: howling
ile: oil
ilka: each, every
ingleneuk: fire place,
    fire side
is na: is not; isn't
ither: other
jaud: headstrong or
    disreputable woman
jaw: billow
jeest: jest
jine: join
jist: just
kail: cabbage
ken: know
kenna: can, may
kent: known
kirk: church
kist: a chest, trunk
kittle: ticklish, touchy
kythe: to make known
laich: low-lying ground; in
    a low tone; inferior
    position
laicher: louder
laird: squire
lancuach: language
    (Gaelic)
lang: long
langheided: level-headed
lat: let
lauch: laugh
lave: rest

leal: loyal
leddy: lady
leein': lying
lees: lies
leme: brightness
leuch: look
levin': lightning
licht: light
lift: sky
lippen: trust, listen
loons: scoundrels, young
men
losh: an expression of
surprise
loun: fellow
loupin': leaping
low: flame
lowse: loose
lugs: ears
luik: look
lum: chimney
mair: more
makar: poet
mappy: bunny
markis: marquis
maukin: hare
maun: must
maunna: must not
mayd: maid
mense: sense
micht: might
mindit: pay mind/heed
mint: hint
misca'd: maligned,
misnamed
mishanter: mishap,
misadventure

mizzer: measure
mochy: mothy
mony: many
mools: earth
moudiwarp: mole
mouls: earth
moutit: molted
muckle: much
mune: moon
murlocks: crumbs
murnin': morning
mutit: muttered
nane: none
nears: kidneys
neb: nose
neebor: neighbor
negus: wine and hot water
with sugar
neip: turnip
neist: next
neuk: nook, corner
nickum: devil
niffer: exchange
noo: now
nor: than
nott: needed
ohn tellt: without telling
ony: any
ony gait: anyhow
ook: week
oot: out
ower: over, too
oxter: armpit
parritch: porridge
pe: be (Gaelic)
pint: point

pit: put
pitawta: potato
pleuch: plow
pleurisy: inflammation in
     the chest
pliskie: prank
poddock: frog
pooch: pouch
poozhonous: poisonous
potty: putty
pree: taste
prent: print
prood: proud
puckle: a few
puir: pure
pur: poor
pyke: pick
quaieter: quieter
quean: wench, hussy
quha: who (Gaelic)
rade: rode
rave/rive: rend, tear
rax: reach
redd: comb
reek: smoke
richt: right (privilege)
rintheroot: cut-throat,
     vagabond
rottans: rodents, rats
royt: riotous
runklin: wrinkling
sae: so
saft: soft
sair: sore
sall: shall
sanna: shan't

sant: saint
sark: shirt
saut: salt
saw: sow
scart: scratch
scaur: cliff
schuil: school
scomfish: suffocate
scoor: scour
scoug: shelter
scrimpit: restricted
scunner: take offense;
     flinch
shackle-bane: wrist
shargar: lean, thin, stunted
     person
shochle: shuffle
shothers: shoulders
shune: shoes
sib: relation
sic, siccan: such
siller: money
sklent: move, dart, fall
skreigh o' day: dawn
smatchit: child
smore: smother, choke
snaw: snow
sneck: lock, latch
snoot: nose, face
sod: sad
sodger: soldier
sookit: sucked at
soord: sword
sough: to be discreetly
     silent
soutar: shoe maker

sowl: soul

spairge: to splash, cause a commotion

spale: wood-shaving

spate: sudden flood

spaud: spade

speir: ask, inquire

speyk: speak

spoony: a foolish person

stane: stone

stank: ditch

steekit: shut

stey: steep

stieve: firm

stook: a shock of grain, pile of sheaves

stour: dust

stown't: stollen it

strathspey: a Highland dance

stravaguin': wandering aimlessly

strive: provoke, bother

sung: singed

suter: shoemaker

sweer: lazy

syne: then

taed: tide

taen, tane: taken

tawn: dawn (Gaelic)

tawse: leather strap

tay: tea; day (Gaelic)

ted: a rowdy person

tent: care

thack: thatch

thae: the

thole: bear

thrown: twisted

till: to

timmer: timber/wood

tint: lost

toom: empty

towie: rope

transe: passage

trews: trousers

tribbles: troubles

trimlin': trembling

tu: too, also

tyke: dog

tyne: lose

ugsome: frightful

uily: oily

uisgebeatha: whiskey (Gaelic)

unco: uncommonly, unusually

versel': yourself

vratch: wretch

wabblet: wobbled

wacht: weight

wad: wager, predict; would

wale: choice

wame: the belly

wantit: wanted

war: were

warl: world

warstlin': wrestling

wat: won't

waur: worse

waurded: spent

weel: well

wha: who

whaur: where
whummle: overturn, overthrow
whups: punishment, whipping
wice: well
wimmen: women
win: to get
winna: wouldn't, won't
wonna: won't
wrocht: wrought
wull: will
wyte: weight; fault
yaird: yard, garden
yer lanes: alone
yett: gate
yird: earth

Bibliography

See John Malcolm Bulloch's "Bibliography of George MacDonald," Aberdeen: The University Press; 1925), for extensive information. It is reprinted in Mary Nance Jordan, *George MacDonald: A Bibliographical Catalog and Record* (Privately published for the Marion E. Wade Collection, Wheaton College, Wheaton, Ill., in Fairfax, Vir., 1984). The following titles have been reprinted in facsimile editions by Johannesen Printing and Publishing, Whitethorn, Calif., 95589. The second date is that of the most recent printings.

Adela Cathcart. [contains many fairy tales, parables, and
   poems] London: Hurst & Blackett, 1864; 1994.
Alec Forbes of Howglen. London: Hurst & Blackett, 1865; 1995.
Annals of a Quiet Neighbourhood. London: Hurst & Blackett,
   1867; 1995.
At the Back of the North Wind. London: Strahan, 1871; 1998.
Castle Warlock. (More often titled *Warlock O'Glenwarlock.*)
   London: Sampson Low, Marston, Searle & Rivington,
   1882; 1998.
David Elginbrod. London: Hurst & Blackett, 1863; 1995.
A Dish of Orts. London: Sampson Low, Marston, & Co. 1893.
Donal Grant. London: Kegan Paul, 1883; 1998.
The Elect Lady. London: Kegan Paul, 1888; 1996.
England's Antiphon. London: Macmillan & Co., 1868; 1996.

Guild Court. London: Hurst & Blackett, 1868; 1992.

Gutta Percha Willie: The Working Genius. London: Henry S.
    King & Co., 1873; 1993.

Heather and Snow. London: Chatto & Windus, 1893; 1996.

Home Again. London: Kegan Paul, 1887; 1992.

The Hope of the Gospel. London: Ward, Lock, Bowden, &
    Co., 1892; 1995.

The Light Princess and Other Fairy Tales. New York: G. P.
    Putnam's Sons, 1893; 1997.

Lilith. London: Chatto & Windus, 1895; published with
    Lilith A, 1998.

Lilith: A Variorum Edition (containing mss. B, C, D, and E).
    2 vols., 1998.

Malcolm. London: Henry S. King & Co., 1875; 1995.

The Marquis of Lossie. London: Hurst & Blackett, 1877; 1995.

Mary Marston. London: Sampson Low, Marston, Searle &
    Rivington, 1881; 1995.

The Miracles of Our Lord. London: Strahan & Co., 1870; 1995.

Paul Faber, Surgeon. London: Hurst & Blackett, 1879; 1998.

Phantastes: A Faerie Romance for Men and Women.
    London: Smith, Elder, 1858; 1998.

The Poetical Works of George MacDonald. 2 vols. London:
    Chatto &Windus, 1893; 1997.

The Portent. London: Smith, Elder, 1864; 1994.

The Princess and Curdie. London: Chatto & Windus,
    1883; 1997.

The Princess and the Goblin. London: Strahan & Co., 1872;
    1997.

Rampolli. London: Longmans, Green & Co., 1897; 1995.

Ranald Bannerman's Boyhood. London: Strahan & Co., 1871;
    1993.

Robert Falconer. London: Hurst & Blackett, 1868; 1995.

A Rough Shaking. London: Blackie & Sons, Ltd., 1891; 1999.

St. George and St. Michael. London: Henry S. King, 1876; 1997.

Salted with Fire. London: Hurst & Blackett, 1897; 1996.

The Seaboard Parish. London: Tinsley Brothers, 1868; 1995.

Sir Gibbie. London: Hurst & Blackett, 1879; 1996.

Stephen Archer and Other Tales. Sampson Low, Marston, Searle & Rivington, 1883; 1994. Published as *The Gifts of the Child Christ*, 1882; Grand Rapids, Mich.: Eerdmans, 1996.

There and Back. London: Kegan Paul, Trench, Trubner & Co., 1891; 1998.

Thomas Wingfold, Curate. London: Hurst & Blackett, 1876; 1997.

The Tragedie of Hamlet. London: Longmans, Green & Co., 1885; 1995.

Unspoken Sermons. London: Alexander Strahan, 1867; 1997.

Unspoken Sermons: Second Series. London: Longmans, Green & Co., 1886; 1997.

Unspoken Sermons: Third Series. London: Longmans, Green & Co., 1889; 1997.

The Vicar's Daughter. London: Tinsley Brothers, 1872; 1998.

Weighed and Wanting. London: Sampson Low, Marston, Searle & Rivington, 1882; 1996.

What's Mine's Mine. London: Kegan Paul, 1886; 1995.

Wilfrid Cumbermede. London: Hurst & Blackett, 1872; 1997.

The Wise Woman. London: Strahan & Co., 1875; 1993.

LETTERS AND ANTHOLOGIES

Hein, Rolland. *The Heart of George MacDonald.* Wheaton, Ill.: Shaw, 1994.

Sadler, Glenn Edward, ed. *An Expression of Character: The Letters of George MacDonald.* Grand Rapids, Mich.: Eerdmans, 1994.

Verploegh, Harry, ed. *3000 Quotations from the Writings of George MacDonald.* Grand Rapids, Mich.: Revel, 1996.

SECONDARY SOURCES

Baker, Joseph Ellis. *The Novel and the Oxford Movement.* Princeton: Princeton University Press, 1932.

Barclay, William. *A Spiritual Autobiography.* Grand Rapids, Mich.: Eerdmans, 1975.

Buckley, Jerome Hamilton. *The Victorian Temper: A Study in Literary Culture.* Cambridge: Harvard University Press, 1951.

Bulloch, John Malcolm. "A Bibliography of George MacDonald." *Aberdeen University Library Bulletin,* 5, No. 30 (February 1925), 679–747.

Fremantle, Anne, ed. *The Visionary Novels of George MacDonald.* New York: Noonday, 1954.

Hetzler, Leo A. "George MacDonald and G.K. Chesterton." *Durham University Journal,* 37 (1976), 176–182.

Hutton, Muriel. "The George MacDonald Collection." *Yale University Library Gazette,* 51 (1976), 74–85.

"Sour Grapeshot: Fault-finding in A *Centennial Bibliography of George MacDonald." Aberdeen University Review,* 41, No. 134 (Autumn 1965), 85–88.

Lewis, C.S. *George MacDonald: An Anthology* London: George Allen & Unwin, 1932.

MacDonald, Ronald. "George MacDonald," *From a Northern Window.* London: James Nisbet, 1911, 55–113.

ABRIDGED AND MODERNIZED NOVELS

The Baron's Apprenticeship (Originally titled *There and Back*),
Bethany House Publishers, Minn., Minn.

The Baronet's Song (*Sir Gibbie*), Bethany House.

The Boyhood of Ranald Bannerman (*Ranald Bannerman's
Boyhood*), Victor Books, Wheaton, Ill.

The Curate's Awakening (*Thomas Wingfold, Curate*), Bethany
House.

A Daughter's Devotion (*Mary Marston*), Bethany House.

The Elect Lady, Victor Books.

The Fisherman's Lady (*Malcolm*), Bethany House.

The Genius of Willie MacMicheal (*Gutta Percha Willie*), Victor
Books.

The Gentlewoman's Choice (*Weighed and Wanting*), Bethany
House.

Heather and Snow, Victor Books.

The Highlander's Last Song (*What's Mine's Mine*), Bethany
House.

Home Again, Victor Books.

The Lady's Confession (*Paul Faber, Surgeon*), Bethany House.

The Laird's Inheritance (*Castle Warlock*), Bethany House.

The Last Castle (*St. George & St. Micheal*), Victor Books.

The Maiden's Bequest (*Alec Forbes of Howglen*), Bethany House.

The Marquis' Secret (*The Marquis of Lossie*), Bethany House.

The Minister's Restoration (*Salted With Fire*), Bethany House.

The Musician's Quest (*Robert Falconer*), Bethany House.

On Tangled Paths (*Weighed and Wanting*), Victor Books.

A Peasant Girl's Dream (*Heather and Snow*), Bethany House.

The Prodigal Apprentice (*Guild Court*), Victor Books.

A Quiet Neighborhood (*Annals of a Quiet Neighborhood*), Victor
Books.

The Seaboard Parish, Victor Books.

The Shepherd's Castle (*Donal Grant*), Bethany House.

The Shopkeeper's Daughter (*Mary Marston*), Victor Books.

The Tutor's First Love (*David Elginbrod*), Bethany House.

The Vicar's Daughter, Victor Books.

The Wanderings of Clare Skymer (*A Rough Shaking*), Victor
   Books.

BIOGRAPHICAL AND CRITICAL STUDIES

Deddo, Gary and Catherine. *George MacDonald: A Devotional
   Guide to His Writings.* Edinburg: Saint Andrew Press,
   1996.

Docherty, John. *The Literary Products of the Lewis
   Carroll–George MacDonald Friendship.* Lewiston: Mellon,
   1995.

Hein, Rolland. *George MacDonald: Victorian Mythmaker.* 1993.
   Whitethorn, Calif.: Johannesen, 1999.

_____. *Christian Mythmakers,* Chicago: Cornerstone
   Press, 1998.

MacDonald, Ronald. *From A Northern Window* (reprint of 1911
   article). Eureka, Calif.: Sunrise Books, 1989.

McGillis, Roderick, ed. *For the Childlike: George MacDonald's
   Fantasies for Children.* Lanham, Md: The Scarecrow
   Press, 1992.

Phillips, Micheal. *George MacDonald, Scotland's Beloved
   Storyteller.* Minneapolis, Minn.: Bethany House
   Publishers, 1987.

Raeper, William. *George MacDonald.* Tring, England: Lion
   Publishing, 1987.

_____, ed. *The Gold Thread: Essays on George*

MacDonald. Edinburgh: University Press, 1990.

Reis, Richard. *George MacDonald's Fiction* (reprint of 1972 edition). Eureka, Calif.: Sunrise Books, 1989.

Robb, Dr. David S. *God's Fiction* (reprint of Scottish edition). Eureka, Calif.: Sunrise Books, Publishers, 1989.

Saintsbury, Elizabeth. *George MacDonald: A Short Life.* Edinburgh, Scotland: Cannongate, 1987.

Triggs, Kathy, George MacDonald: The Seeking Heart, Basingstoke, England: Pickering & Inglis, 1984.

_____. The Stars and the Stillness. Cambridge, England: Lutherworth Press, 1986.

Index